Moruroa
Blues

Reed's Maritime Library

Moruroa Blues

Lynn Pistoll

SHERIDAN HOUSE

This edition published 2001 by
Sheridan House Inc.
145 Palisade Street
Dobbs Ferry, New York 10522
www.sheridanhouse.com

First published in Great Britain 2001
by Thomas Reed Publications

A Cataloging-in-Publication record of this book is available
from the Library of Congress, Washington, DC.

Edited by Alex Milne
Series Consultant Tony Brunton-Reed
Design & Layout by C E Marketing
Produced by Omega Profiles Ltd.
Printed and bound in Great Britain

ISBN 1-57409-140-9

Dedication

To my three sons:
Barrett, Chance and Tobyn

Also to David McTaggart, who died in a car accident
in Italy just as this book was going to press.
David was a true veteran for world peace, an astute sailor
and the person who inspired me to act on my beliefs.
God rest his soul.

FOREWORD

by US Congressman Eni F. H. Faleomavaega

In June 1995, French President Jacques Chirac announced that France would explode eight more nuclear bombs in the South Pacific, beginning September 1995. Having already detonated more than 187 nuclear bombs in this region, France's intent to resume nuclear testing here, in violation of the 1992 world moratorium, caused deep outrage and alarm in the region and in the world community.

In a firestorm of international outrage, government after government spoke out in opposition. US Congressmen and Senators supported resolutions condemning the resumption of testing. Demonstrations involving tens of thousands of protesters took place in French Polynesia and around the globe.

Ordinary citizens all over the world responded, and the story of some of those responses is told with simple eloquence by Lynn Pistoll in *Moruroa Blues*. The book chronicles the voyage of a New Zealand vessel, the *Joie*, which travelled to Moruroa to protest French nuclear testing. In words sometimes angry, sometimes humorous, the skipper of the *Joie* documents the story – from the decision in July, 1995 to sail to French Polynesia to the return to Auckland in November of that year – of ordinary people who stood up to a nuclear power and said "Enough!"

On September 5 1995, despite international pleadings, protests and appeals from the peoples of the Pacific and other world leaders, France exploded an atomic bomb with a nuclear punch of 20 kilotons at Moruroa atoll. Sixty miles away, on the island of Tureia, Pacific island children splashed and played in the ocean waves from that blast.

The world knew why France exploded its bombs in

French Polynesia and not in France. No one wants to subject their homeland, their children, to this danger if they have a choice.

Historically, the people of the Pacific have had little choice. Nuclear nations have consistently treated Pacific islanders and their way of life as expendable. In 1954, the US detonated a 15-megaton thermonuclear bomb, over a thousand times more powerful than the Hiroshima bomb, on Bikini Atoll. Marshall Islanders living on nearby Rongelap and Utirik atolls believe they were used as guinea pigs for US nuclear radiation experiments.

France's story was well-scripted and presented through the international wire services. But the people of the Pacific have our own story to tell. It is a travesty that our voices have been muted and our concerns have been marginalized by world leaders who espouse the principles of democracy from the pulpit of the Enlightenment.

And that is why I am so happy that my good friend Lynn has finally finished his book. Because his book tells the story of a moment in time when ordinary people from all over the world joined together, side-by-side with Pacific people, to let France know that the testing had to stop, that the nuclear madness had to stop.

Moruroa Blues is an inspiring account of how effective the voices of ordinary people can be when they are raised in a just cause. As a member of both the Pacific Island community and the US House of Representatives, as one who sailed to the nuclear testing site at Moruroa and was arrested at the hands of French commandos in the very waters that the god Taaroa gave to the people of Polynesia, I know firsthand the story told in this book, and I urge everyone who dares to hope for a nuclear-free world to read it.

Lynn should be commended for being there at Moruroa to stand with the people of the Pacific. He should also be commended for documenting the story. Because of his book, the story will be told, and because of his book we will never forget the lesson that *Moruroa Blues* teaches us – if enough people join their hearts and minds for peace, powerful things can be accomplished.

INTRODUCTION

Moruroa Blues is the story of ordinary people taking on the might of the French Government and its military. It begins in June of 1995 when French President Jacques Chirac decided to resume nuclear testing in the South Pacific. Shortly after the announcement, 14 yachts with their skippers and crew joined the New Zealand Peace Flotilla. With only 6 weeks' notice, and against strong odds, they managed to arrange finance, quit their jobs, prepare their vessels and sail some 3000 nautical miles in some of the world's roughest waters to protest against the French resumption of nuclear testing.

The account reveals the inside story of the protest from the view of a single peace flotilla skipper. It covers the struggle, challenges and achievement of organising and preparing for the venture, sailing in the Roaring Forties during winter, and contesting the 12-mile Exclusion Zone at Moruroa. The campaign focused world-wide attention on the French programme, which ultimately resulted in the signing of the South Pacific Nuclear-Free Zone and the Comprehensive Test Ban Treaty and the ending of five decades of testing by the nuclear powers.

Although some time has passed since the 1995/96 protest campaign, I feel strongly that the event is of historical interest and should be placed on permanent record. The story of Moruroa and French Polynesia is not over; it has barely begun. With what has to be hundreds of 'Chernobyls' created under Moruroa, it will continue to be a 'hot spot' for generations to come.

The story is my personal account of the adventure as skipper of the *Joie*, the longest-staying New Zealand Peace Flotilla yacht, returning to Moruroa a second time from Papeete and finally closing off the protest campaign with the Greenpeace yacht *Caramba* on 27 October 1995.

I was personally inspired by this commitment of ordinary people and by the flotilla working as a team to denounce the French nuclear testing at Moruroa. I was also motivated by what I had learnt about past French Government activities on the islands of Moruroa and Fangataufa, as well as its general colonial rule of French Polynesia.

As the major source for the story I have used the ship's log and my personal diary. I have also used the diary of Dennis Johnson, the first mate of the *Joie*, as well as conversations with other skippers and crew involved in the protest campaign, media reports and other printed materials. The facts, figures and events in this book I believe to be true; however, due to the secrecy surrounding the French tests and general unavailability of information, verification of some is difficult. I have endeavoured to present a general account of the protest; however, there were many other boats and people involved, and many other events and experiences took place which are not fully or accurately presented in this story. Undoubtedly others (particularly the French Government and military) will have their own perspective of events.

Throughout the book I have used the words 'French' and 'France' to mean the French Government, colonial administrators of French Polynesia, or the French military. They are not intended to mean the ordinary French people or the country of France.

Acknowledgments

The New Zealand Peace Flotilla mission could not have been accomplished without the help of many New Zealand companies and ordinary citizens. They supported the effort through financial donations, donations of provisions and equipment, their own personal time and, most importantly, their spirits. I would like to thank all those companies and individuals who made donations to the flotilla.

Much praise is extended to Tony Atkinson and his team at the Auckland Peace Flotilla Office for their professional and highly devoted effort in fundraising and organising and administering the protest. Likewise, many thanks to Dennis Johnson, campaign co-ordinator for the Wellington Peace Flotilla Office, and his team, who organised substantial financial and other support.

Literally hundreds of people contributed directly to the support and preparation of the Wellington Peace Flotilla vessels. I would like to acknowledge them all here but I fear I will miss someone, which would be a great embarrassment. Instead, I would like to bestow my gratitude to all those who helped in any way with the campaign. You know who you all are. Well done! Please accept my sincere appreciation and thanks.

I would like to acknowledge the other Peace Flotilla skippers and crew who committed their boats, finance and souls. Without them there would have been no Peace Flotilla. I would especially like to thank the other Wellington boats and crew with whom we shared so much time and energy. Also I would like to acknowledge Greenpeace who were instrumental in organising campaign activities at Moruroa and Papeete and who provided what support they could.

Thanks also to the New Zealand Government for its political support and the provision of the navy research ship *Tui* on location at Moruroa. The ship and crew provided substantial moral and other support, and a sense of 'home security' which was vital to the mission.

Much gratitude is extended to Nikao Radio in Rarotonga and the New Zealand Ham Radio Association who organised the flotilla roll-call and set up a radio network across New Zealand which allowed the flotilla to communicate with their families back home. It was a tremendous effort and highly appreciated by the flotilla.

I would like to personally thank my crew (Dennis Johnson, Paul McMaster, Paul Giles, John Frost and Ingrid Gordon) for their commitment, enduring strength, resilience and resolve throughout the campaign, and for putting up with their skipper for such a long period!

Finally I would like to thank all the people who encouraged and helped me to write and publish this story, especially Sue Dahl, Alastair Lovett, Chris and Susan Couryner, Warren Pickett and Helen Forlong who helped edit the book, and Greenpeace New Zealand who provided access to their news releases and other information.

CHAPTER 1

Log, 27 October 1995

*B*OOM! *We are 2 miles from the 12-mile Exclusion Zone at Moruroa. I am inside the* Joie *playing the guitar when I hear and feel a prolonged shuddering. I shout to Dennis and Ingrid, who are on deck, "What the hell was that?" They say it was probably the sun awning flapping in the wind. Fifteen minutes later Daniel from the Greenpeace vessel Caramba calls us on the VHF radio to confirm that it was a 60-kilotonne underground nuclear explosion (four times the size of Hiroshima). It was France's third explosion in this test series. "Shame on France, shame on France, shame on France," is the only thing I can think to say back to Daniel on the radio. I know that the French military will be listening to our conversation.*

Dennis is now sitting on deck in complete silence, a very stricken and sad expression over his face. In fact everyone is completely quiet now as we ponder the situation. We have been at sea now for nearly 2 months. We have endured many hardships and obstacles to protest against this test series. The hurricane season is upon us. We must leave. We must now return to New Zealand.

Getting Hooked

The whole thing began for me around the first of July 1995 when I saw a '60 minutes' programme on television. The show featured an interview with David McTaggart, a founding director of Greenpeace, who was coming out of retirement to vehemently protest against the French resumption of nuclear testing in the South Pacific.

David McTaggart was furious with the announcement by the French that they were breaking the moratorium on nuclear testing that they signed in 1992. French President Chirac had announced that they would be testing another eight nuclear devices on the atoll island of Moruroa in French Polynesia. In announcing the resumption of testing, he made three concessions: testing would cease after eight new tests; France would sign a Comprehensive Test Ban Treaty (CTBT); and no new weapons systems would be developed.

Looking very frail on television, McTaggart admitted he was no longer a spring chicken but this was very important to him, and the world, and he would be sailing to the atoll to protest against the planned tests. He spoke with great passion, sincerity and dedication to the cause. I was moved by him, and when he said, 'Come on you New Zealanders, get your boats together and join us at Moruroa', an indescribable sensation ran through my body. Goosebumps tingled my skin, moisture crept into my eyes and a feeling of warmth grew from deep within me. 'I'd like to be able to do this,' I mumbled to myself.

The sensations quickly faded with the realisation of the many obstructions and other commitments that seemed insurmountable. These included work, family, money and the current state of readiness of my vessel *Joie*, a Cascade 42-foot sloop. *Joie* had not sailed off-shore for over 14 years.

The thought of sailing to Moruroa kept brewing inside me and was constantly being perked up by all the media reports, including New Zealand and world-wide political opposition to the French plans. The announcement provoked a wave of international condemnation and fears that it could set back efforts for a global test ban treaty.

The Treaty on the Non-proliferation of Nuclear Weapons (NPT) came into force in 1970. Under the terms of the treaty, the nuclear states agreed to eliminate their nuclear weapons. In return, the non-nuclear states agreed not to manufacture or acquire nuclear weapons. At the time, stopping all nuclear testing through a CTBT was seen as a key step to stopping and reversing the arms race.

The final decision of the NPT Review and Extension Conference in New York in May 1995 was that the nuclear states should exercise the 'utmost restraint' on nuclear testing until a comprehensive test ban was completed no later than 1996. Only a month following the conference, France announced a series of tests as intensive as any it had conducted at the height of the Cold War.

New Zealand's response was very strong, and the Opposition backed the Government's decision to freeze defence links and ministerial contacts with France.

In announcing the freeze, Prime Minister Jim Bolger asked why the new French President was determined to begin his presidency by ignoring the wishes of countries like Australia and New Zealand, which had sent thousands of young men to fight for France in two wars. Relations between France and New Zealand had been slowly returning to normal 10 years after the French bombing of the *Rainbow Warrior* in Auckland Harbour.

Other nations also made statements in response to Chirac's announcement, and most opposed the resumption of French testing:

Australian Prime Minister Paul Keating: 'The Government has decided to freeze co-operation between Australia and France in the defence field at its existing level while any new testing programme continues.'

Japanese Prime Minister Tomiichi Murayama: 'The French decision seriously betrays the trust of non-nuclear states.'

French Polynesia Territorial Senator Daniel Millaud: Mr Millaud called the move 'a monumental error that is going to pose a lot of problems for the French nation and Polynesia'.

Main opposition leader Boris Leontieff also condemned France for not consulting the territory over the resumption of testing.

South Pacific Forum: The 15-country South Pacific Forum strongly condemned France's decision, saying it showed a 'flagrant disregard for world and regional opinion'.

European Parliament: The European Parliament passed an emergency resolution stating that European Union nations were 'shocked by the decision of French President Chirac' and urged France to reconsider its decision.

Cook Islands Marine Resources Minister Tepure Tapaitau: He was 'both concerned and opposed to nuclear testing resuming, especially if research shows it will affect our waters'.

United States: A White House spokesman said that the US was disappointed. 'The United States has suspended its own nuclear testing and we hoped that all other nuclear powers would do so as well.'

Canadian Foreign Affairs spokesman Rodney Moore: He condemned France's decision but said Canada was encouraged by Mr Chirac's 'personal commitment to a definitive end to France's testing by May 1996 at the latest'.

British Foreign Office: A spokesman said, 'We see no reason why a limited programme of tests need affect the prospects of a successful negotiation of a comprehensive test ban treaty.'

The relatively weak responses from the United States and Britain led analysts to suggest that they were in cahoots with France. One could imagine the likely scenario: support of the French resumption of testing in exchange for the fissile material data obtained from the detonations. This data could then be used in US and British nuclear computer simulation programmes.

My aspirations about going to Moruroa were again sparked by news of an Auckland yacht, *Triptych*, which would sail to the atoll. *Triptych* was a 65-foot trimaran owned by a Manukau city councillor, Barry Keon, who invited other vessels to join him. It occurred to me that Mr Keon's intentions may have had an element of political profiteering but, nevertheless, he had kicked off the concept of a New

Zealand Peace Flotilla, which started a landslide of interest and publicity.

In the second week of July, while returning to my home on board *Joie*, I noticed Jon Tucker and Nick Gales working feverishly on the Chaffers Marina pier. They were cutting up plywood, and saw-horses, sawdust, power and hand tools were scattered all over the pier. The odd thing about this activity was that it was nearly dusk on a typical cold, windy and rainy Wellington winter day.

Curious about what they were up to, I wandered down the pier towards them. I knew Jon and Nick only in a casual sense from walking past them on the dock. Jon appeared to be an alternative lifestyle person with over-grown hair, a dark bushy beard and a welcoming smile. Nick, on the other hand, was clean-cut and tidily dressed, looking like a bureaucrat after a busy day at the office. 'What do these two have in common?' I thought as I approached them.

"Hello, what are you guys up to?" I asked, as the strong cold Wellington south wind pierced my clothing. Jon explained that they were building additional water tanks for his boat. "We're going to Moruroa to protest against the French nuclear tests," he said. "Cool!", I replied, and in the same breath without thinking at all I added, "I'd like to go as well." I must have sounded fairly sure of myself, because Jon immediately accepted my verbal application, and the planning began. 'What have I got myself into?' I thought. 'Will I be able to pull this thing off?'

Jon, who had been a peace activist for many years, was very clued up on recent developments regarding the Peace Flotilla. He explained that there were two groups organising to go to Moruroa. One was an Australian effort organised by Lindsay Chinnery, which had already received a sponsorship proposal from the GoodLife Corporation, and the other was Barry Keon's, for which a trust was being formed in Auckland to raise funds for the flotilla. Jon and Nick said that there should be about $25,000 available for each boat that would be going. This helped alleviate my concern on the finance front but I was still sceptical about the funds actually materialising.

I went back to my boat and dug out the pilot charts and other information I had on the South Pacific Ocean. A quick survey showed that such a voyage, to be undertaken in winter, required an easterly run of over 2000 nautical miles in the southern latitude between 35 and 41° before bearing north for a further 800 nautical miles into the relatively benign waters of the subtropics: a trip of almost 3000 nautical miles. The pilot charts forecast a daunting frequency of storms and gales. A look through the texts on planning ocean passages clearly revealed that winter was no time to make such a journey.

The next morning, Jon knocked on my boat and told me that Hank Schouten of the Wellington Evening Post was coming down to interview us and photograph the three Wellington yachts and crew going to Moruroa. At that point, the crew and boats considering going were: Jon Tucker, his wife Barbara and the younger three of their five sons (Daniel, Sam and Matthew) on the 46-foot Hereshoff-designed gaff ketch *New Zealand Maid*; Nick and Cathy Gales, their 7-year-old son Jeremy and 2-year-old daughter Jemma, on the 54-foot ketch *Kela*; and myself on the 42-foot sloop *Joie*, with no crew at that point.

The interviews were held on *New Zealand Maid*. Nick and I were very apprehensive about the potential news coverage, and told Hank Schouten that a condition of his interviews was that his article explain we were only in the planning stages of the voyage and that the three boats would only be going if we could meet the large financial and other demands of the venture. He agreed. The article and picture of the crew, perched on the bow of *New Zealand Maid*, appeared on the front page of the Evening Post. This marked the beginning of the onslaught of journalists from the press, radio and television.

We had less than 6 weeks to get our boats ready to go. We registered our interests with both the Australian and Auckland trusts but got no commitment from them for the expected funds.

The Australian trust was trying to organise a race to Moruroa and the press reported that as many as 80 vessels would be participating from Australia. This seemed to me an amazingly large number of boats.

Meanwhile, the Auckland–based Barry Keon effort,

reported to have the support of 40 boats going from New Zealand, appeared disorganised as a flotilla movement, and focused most of its energy on Keon's own vessel, *Triptych*. A number of peace activists under the leadership of Tony Atkinson, who had previously sailed to Moruroa to protest against French testing in 1987, took over the flotilla operation. They established their organisation at the Ponsonby Cruising Club in Auckland, enlisted a number of volunteers and began fundraising and other official Peace Flotilla activities.

CHAPTER 2

French Nuclear Testing in the Pacific

Before sailing to Moruroa it was relevant to consider exactly what we were attempting to put a stop to. Under General de Gaulle, the French Government commenced their nuclear programme in the mid-1950s. They conducted their first tests in the Sahara desert, in the French colony of Algeria, between 1960 and 1966. However, after Algeria fought its way to independence, the French were expelled; furthermore, a miscalculation of weather conditions could have sent fallout over Europe.

The only other suitable French territory for testing was the Tuamotu group in French Polynesia. They moved quickly to build airports, bases, wharves and testing facilities and, at the peak of the infiltration, employed about 7000 military personnel there with as many sailors living on ships. This was all done with little or no consultation or agreement with the local indigenous population and neighbouring island countries. The French Government reassured the islanders that the proposed testing posed no health risks and that everyone would benefit from the subsequent economic spin-off.

And economic spin-off there was. Remembering that French Polynesia was only a small Pacific Island economy with around 85 000 inhabitants spread among 130 or so islands, the French military programme had a profound impact.

Up until the 1960s the life and economy of French Polynesia was largely one of subsistence farming and fishing, with modest amounts of cash cropping (copra, vanilla, etc.). Since the mid 1960s, however, the way of life had been utterly

WESTERN
SAMOA

VANUATU

FIJI

TONGA

Auckland

NORTH
ISLAND

NEW
ZEALAND

Wellington

SOUTH
ISLAND

CHATHAM
ISLANDS

COOK
ISLANDS

TUAMOTU ISLANDS

GAMBIER ISLANDS

Papeete
MOOREA TAHITI

VANAVANA TUREIA

RAROTONGA

MORUROA

RAPA

SOUTH PACIFIC
OCEAN

0   500   1000 Kilometres
0   500   1000 Nautical Miles

transformed: The local subsistence and cash-crop economy had collapsed and there had been extensive migration from the outer islands to Tahiti, and from the remote regions of Tahiti itself to the capital, Papeete. There had been an artificial overgrowth of the public and private service ('tertiary') sector. About 80 percent of the territory's workforce was salaried (as opposed to self-reliant), with most of these jobs created either directly or indirectly by the nuclear testing programme and the military presence in Polynesia.

When the French first moved in, the cost of building bases, operating all their planes and warships and maintaining all the troops had originally been estimated at 1000 million French francs. Within a year the actual expenses exceeded 2500 million francs. Less than a year later the official figure was 6000 million (approaching US $1 billion).

The French Government had contributed to building a 'false economy' in French Polynesia. One has only to sail 300 nautical miles to the Cook Islands to find that prices for nearly all commodities and services are less than a third of the price in Papeete. The dramatic development of all levels of infrastructure in Tahiti, as well as the relatively high per capita GNP, cannot be sustainable beyond the existence of the nuclear testing programme without continued subsidies. The prosperity of Polynesia had been almost 90 percent dependent on money from France.

The French CEP (Centre for Experiments in the Pacific) favoured the island atoll of Moruroa for the planned open air testing because of its remote location, exceptionally wide pass through the coral reef, and lagoon deep enough to harbour huge ships safely. They were advised by the French Polynesia Territorial Assembly (the ruling body of the islands) that Moruroa was territorial land and could not be sold or leased without their express consent. Local French Commanders ignored this and moved into Moruroa promptly and therefore illegally. This perhaps explains one error that has been maintained by the French ever since; they misspelled the name of the atoll as 'Mururoa', whereas the true name, familiar to native islanders, has always been 'Moruroa'.

An airstrip, base and wharves were soon constructed there. The Foreign Legionnaires next blasted a huge hole in the coral ring on the neighbouring island of Fangataufa and built another wharf and airstrip there.

The atoll island of Hao, 200 nautical miles north-west of Moruroa, became a large airstrip and army base where 2000 soldiers lived. The bombs and materials would arrive and be assembled on Hao. The peaceful local Polynesian population of 800 people had no say about the intrusion. Accommodation and recreational facilities were also built in and around Papeete. These facilities accommodated up to 7000 soldiers, half on a full-time basis and the other half on a rotating basis.

Although it is well documented that the Local Territorial Assembly, comprised of native Polynesian leaders, tried in vain to stop the planned French testing programme, they were simply politically outwitted, ignored and overruled by the French Government.

On 2 July 1966, the first Pacific nuclear test was conducted above Moruroa and, in September, President de Gaulle visited French Polynesia to witness the detonation of a 120-kilotonne device, the most powerful French atomic bomb to date.

Unfortunately, the wind was from the east and a nuclear explosion would threaten the islands to the west of Moruroa with fallout. After two frustrating days waiting for the wind direction to shift, President de Gaulle ordered the device to be detonated regardless.

Four days later, alarming levels of radioactive fallout were detected in the rainwater in Western Samoa, 2000 nautical miles downwind, and in the Cook Islands and Fiji. The amount of radioactive fallout in French Polynesia, very much closer to the explosion, has never been revealed by French authorities. The French Government had not informed them of the blast or the potential dangers.

In 1968, France conducted its first thermonuclear (hydrogen bomb) tests. The yields were far greater than from previous tests. The first test, conducted at Fangataufa on 24 August, had a yield of 2.6 megatonnes, more than 170 times Hiroshima, and this was an open air test. The contamination put Fangataufa off-limits for humans for the next 6 years. Even today, the French military does not allow its workers to stay there for extended periods.

From 1966 to 1974, the French conducted around 44 atmospheric tests on Moruroa and Fangataufa. International protests intensified. France was condemned at the International Court of Justice in the Hague, and the UN and Pacific and Latin American Governments took diplomatic measures, some withdrawing their ambassadors from France. Finally, in 1974, under growing international public opinion, French President Giscard d'Estaing decided to transfer the tests underground.

From 1975 to 1992, the French conducted a total of 143 underground tests on Moruroa and Fangataufa.

In 1973, when the New Zealand Labour Government became frustrated by the French refusal to abandon nuclear testing, it decided to make a visible protest by sending the Leander-class frigate *Otago* to the scene. Onboard were 243 sailors, five news media representatives and Fraser Colman, a Cabinet Minister. Accompanying *Otago* was a private protest fleet, and together they infuriated the French to the extent that they declared a 72 mile limit in international waters around the atoll. Prime Minister Norman Kirk ordered *Otago* to ignore the 72-mile limit and to sail to the edge of the 12-mile zone. The French then rammed some of the protest boats when they tried to get closer.

In April 1992, in the name of arms control and under growing international pressure, French socialist President François Mitterand suspended the underground test series at Moruroa. Over the 32-year period of testing, France had conducted 187 nuclear tests. It was an open secret that a seven-man committee, appointed by Mitterand and including defence experts, recommended testing be resumed.

Jacques Chirac, a Gaullist, had been Prime Minister when France tested weapons in the 1970s and 1980s. Upon taking Presidency, he soon announced the resumption of testing "to ensure the reliability and security of France's nuclear arsenal and to perfect laboratory simulation to make further tests unnecessary."

New Zealand first learned of France's decision to resume testing through the news media.

The last series had been cut short by socialist President

Mitterrand, and Chirac was determined to finish it and press on with strengthening France's nuclear deterrent capability.

When Mitterrand called a halt to the testing in 1992, it was known that the French Atomic Energy Authority treated the suspension with great hostility and argued that more explosions were necessary to understand the technical limitations of alternatives to testing, ensure the reliability of existing stockpiles, and verify the performance of the new M45, M5 and ASLP missile warheads. But times had changed and specialists suggested that the primary purpose of the French test series appeared to be to modernise its arsenal, including miniaturisation technology. The modernisation of France's air and water nuclear deterrent capability fitted nicely with Chirac's plan to eliminate 18 strategic nuclear missiles in Albion in Southern France.

Chirac needed to conduct eight nuclear explosions of varying intensity and character to capture the necessary fissile material data. With this data, he was able to simulate all the tests he wanted and develop all the new weapons alternatives his army needed. He could do so quietly, in the privacy of his laboritories, without the menace of protesters or the responsibility of public accountability.

Chirac boldly stated that, after the last eight tests, France would quit for good and sign the CTBT. Quit for good? The data collected may keep its politicians happy for several years, but what when it's time to take the nuclear race up another notch or in another direction?

The French Nuclear Development Programme:

1945	Set up the CEA (Atomic Energy Commission)
1960–66	Algeria: four atmospheric and 13 underground tests
1962	Set up the CEP (Centre for Experiments in the Pacific)
1966–74	Moruroa and Fangataufa, 44 atmospheric tests
1975–92	Moruroa and Fangataufa, 143 underground tests
1992	Mitterrand suspends testing
1995–96	Chirac resumes testing at Moruroa and Fangataufa. Six of the planned eight tests conducted

After the NPT was signed in 1970, France increased its
nuclear arsenal from around 50 to approximately 500 weapons
and continued to modernise its nuclear arsenal.

CHAPTER 3

The Campaign Trail

I asked myself, 'Why am I doing this? Why did I commit to what appears to be an almost impossible task of raising money, getting *Joie* outfitted, quitting work and sailing all the way to Moruroa for an indefinite period of protest? I must be nuts or something.' I had never protested against anything in my whole life, except perhaps when my mother wanted to cut my hair!

I searched for the answer. In a philosophical sense, it was a complex question. I looked at myself, age 43, and asked, 'All the time that you have been on planet Earth, what have you done for the good of mankind?' I tried to think of something. Well, there was that time, when cruising in Mexico, I gave a box of .22 bullets to some young Mexicans. I thought they would use them to hunt for rabbits, to provide food for their families, but I saw them later in the day on the beach shooting seagulls for fun! Then there was the time I gave my mandolin away to a Polynesian in the Marquesas. We were playing music together, and he had never seen a mandolin. Did this count?

It is a funny world, especially the capitalist world. It is a very selfish place where everyone fends for themselves. You grow up, go to school, then get a job, a house, a family, and all the time you look after just yourself and your family: 'Who cares about the neighbours, or the rest of the world? We have enough problems of our own.' We then pick up the paper and read about all the problems in the world: pollution, congestion, oil spills, depleting ozone layer, population explosions, starvation, crime and civil wars. 'Why can't they get their act together?' we ask.

The last time I was in a traffic jam, I caught myself saying, 'This is disgusting! Look at all these cars plugging up my way.' I looked over to the next car, and saw an unhappy person mumbling as well. He was probably saying the same thing about me. There is no question in my mind that everyone contributes a little to the environmental and social problems that we have today and everyone should therefore take a little time to make a contribution to fixing something.

There are about 6 billion people living in the world. If each person on average spent only 2 hours a month working on an environmental or social problem of their choice, this would result in 144 billion hours of work, or a full-time equivalent workforce of 75 000 people. With this sort of human capital, providing it could be managed properly, we would be well down the track of making our planet Earth a better place to live. So why don't we do this? Was this why I was going to Moruroa? No, not really. It had more to do with the fact that I don't care much for nuclear bombs, nor the French Government, and I love sailing!

I still had a vivid memory of the late 1970s, at the peak of the Cold War, when I was living aboard *Joie* in Harris Harbour, Juneau, Alaska. One day an announcement came over the radio... 'This morning, China detonated a nuclear device and the radioactive cloud is expected to drift over the state of Alaska. We advise all people to stay indoors, and to close your windows and doors.' This totally blew me away. Here we were, sitting at the edge of a wilderness, and some stupid person in China set off a nuclear bomb that threatened our environment.

How could this be? China was some 6000 nautical miles to the west of us, and we were receiving the fallout. This really worried me. Things weren't the best between Russia and the United States. In fact, both countries had scores of ballistic missiles aimed at each other and political commentators of the day were saying that the chance of at least a 'limited nuclear confrontation' was high. So there I was, sitting in the middle of the potential war zone. If the Yanks got the Russians first then, because of the prevailing wind patterns, we would end up with the fallout. And if the Russians got us first, well that would be that. What a dismal situation: the strong potential for a war, and I would get snuffed no matter who eventually won.

This single event played a major part in my migration to

New Zealand in 1981. It also taught me to be a staunch sceptic of the merits of nuclear deterrence programmes.

With only 4 weeks to go before the required departure date, Nick, Jon and I became concerned about the likelihood of any guaranteed funding from the two flotilla groups. Also, the inundation of the media was absorbing our valuable preparation time. We decided we needed to form our own Wellington-based flotilla campaign to make sure that we were able to finance the trip. We needed help.

Jon Tucker resigned from his teaching position and Nick successfully negotiated 10 weeks leave from his employer, the New Zealand Department of Conservation, where he worked as a marine mammal research scientist. I was self-employed with my own small market consulting practice, so it was easy to negotiate with myself for extended leave!

We consulted Nicky Hager, long-time Wellington-based peace activist. He agreed to come to a meeting and recommended we call Wairarapa-based Dennis Johnson to assist in the campaign fund raising. We talked to Dennis on the telephone that evening. He was excited about the prospect of helping out and said he would meet us at the marina the next morning around 10 a.m.

The next morning, glancing out the porthole of *Joie*, I saw a man in his early 50s, balding, with the remaining bits of his hair tied neatly back in a small pony tail. He was wearing a necklace of some sort as well as a colourful handkerchief tied around his neck, and was carrying an Indian knitted bag as his brief case. I thought this guy looked like some left-over flower power type from the 60s. He was looking around as if a bit lost.

I popped my head out of the boat and asked, "Hello, are you Dennis Johnson by any chance?" "Yes I am," he said. "And you must be one of the flotilla boats, the 'Joe-ee'," he said as he read the name on the back of the boat. "Yes that's right. The name of the boat is actually pronounced 'Jaa-waa'. It's a French word," I said. "Oh right," Dennis said. He tried again, 'Joe-wee.' That was close enough for now, I thought, and said, "let me introduce you to the other boats and skippers", and I walked with him down the pier.

The three skippers and crew, Nicky Hager and Dennis

sat down in the galley of *Kela* for an exciting meeting that lasted nearly 6 hours. Jon briefed everyone on the status of the Auckland and Australian flotilla efforts. He cited three confirmed boats likely to participate and several 'probables', far fewer than the 100 that were reported in the news.

Nicky Hager gave valuable advice on how to organise an appeal, how to harness the help of the Wellington-based peace movement and how to successfully work with the media. We agreed to form our own Wellington-based trust, and the protocols for its operation. Dennis, who revealed his enthusiasm to participate in the Peace Flotilla from the start, naively accepted the position of Wellington Peace Flotilla Spokesman and Campaign Co-ordinator. Congratulations Dennis, and thanks mate!

After the meeting, the other skippers and I felt a tremendous relief from the pressure. We could now get on with the important jobs of readying our boats for the long voyage and dealing with our personal affairs, for which we had only 4 weeks. Thankfully, we now had the structure of a fundraising organisation in place and a person to drive it: Dennis. It was ironic, as Dennis hated money!

Dennis was born and raised in a small town called Taihape, near the centre of the North Island. Know as 'Gumboot Capital of the World', Taihape is a town which is the subject of many New Zealand jokes. It is often referred to as a 'hole in the wall' town, appearing from nowhere, near the foothills of the Tongariro mountain range, where the major entertainment might be sight-seeing the vehicles on State Highway 1 which were forced to pass through it! It is a cold and wet place: gumboot territory, with an economy supported by tough, hard-working New Zealand farmers. Taihape actually hosts an annual gumboot throwing competition. No doubt many of Dennis's personal attributes were shaped by this unique birth place.

Upon my initial meeting with Dennis, he appeared to be a simple, genuine and modest man who was highly concerned with nuclear environmental issues. I learned that he had been involved in the peace movement for nearly 30 years and had got his start when New Zealand proposed nuclear power plants for the country. He said he just had to do something to stop all that nonsense. He was emotional, strongly philosophical, articulate and stubbornly committed to his beliefs. And most important of all, he was very enthusiastic with the prospect of helping to 'stick it to the Frogs'. I liked his attitude!

Being a fireman from Masterton, about 120 kilometres north of Wellington, Dennis seemed to have the flexibility to juggle his shifts around to get some temporary time off. He went home that evening, sorted out his affairs, packed his bags and arrived back at the marina a day later raring to get going with his new challenge. The only problem was that there was no place to go.

There was no flotilla office, not even a phone for Dennis to use and he became very frustrated, exhibiting anxiety similar to a dog with a T-bone steak just out of its reach. He tried a number of options for an office, including approaching Lambton Harbour Management. They were slow in responding, and even Telecom said it would take a few days to install a phone.

Everything was moving far too slowly for Dennis. His anxiety increased. Fortunately, I had some spare room in my small office in town and suggested that he set up there to get things going.

Dennis moved into my office on 26 July. He now had some place to call home: a desk, chair, and telephone. The planning and organisation were firmly under way.

The first priority was the campaign kick-off event planned for Monday, 1 August. An earlier meeting with a local Wellington radio station, Newstalk ZB, was promising and they agreed to help us with our fund-raising efforts. The station planned to broadcast its popular Lindsay Yeo Breakfast Show from the yachts at Chaffers Marina.

To complement the show, we began planning to pull *Joie* out of the water and place her in front of the French Embassy on Jervois Quay, decked out with banners. We felt this would be the most effective way to let French President Jacques Chirac know that we were coming. It would serve as a bloody good publicity stunt as well, we thought.

By the end of the day we had obtained Wellington City Council approval to park *Joie* in front of the Embassy. 'All right, things are happening!'

After what seemed to be an endless string of phone calls, Dennis managed to arrange a donation of 150 empty buckets to use for collecting money, but was unsuccessful in getting council approval for street collections. To get approval, we had to be a charitable non-profit organisation. When overhearing Dennis's conversation with the council employee responsible for street collections, I broke into tears of laughter. "Isn't saving the world charitable?" Dennis asked. Dennis politely and calmly finished the conversation by saying, "Well, I hope that in 2000 years there are still some charitable organisations around."

We made a decision to proceed with the street appeal regardless.

In a matter of a couple of days, Dennis managed to build his support group for the campaign. He enlisted the support of people in the peace movement, including Gunda Tente and John Warren, and his personal friend Ken Anderson, who all helped immensely with the street appeal as well as other activities.

Rozellia Mawhinney and Cham Keel also volunteered their help. Many street collectors, including students, joined in, and before long our little office was a hive of activity.

I put a sign on the door that read: Headquarters for the Wellington to Moruroa Peace Flotilla. Gunda, who was of German ancestry, commented about my choice of word 'headquarters'. She said it sounded very militaristic, which she thought was appropriate for this particular peace mission.

Dennis soon had all the press, radio and television contacts sorted out and was calling them, going to live interviews and firing off press releases right and left.

Perhaps stemming from his upbringing in Taihape, he was a technophobe. Rather than use the personal computer, he preferred to hand-write his press releases for each station, or news outlet. The fax machine, which he was inclined to use, became his worst enemy. He could not properly use this modern day machine. He did major battle with it; he moaned incessantly about it; he was afraid of it. It was a constant source of irritation to him.

I approached former Prime Minister and Member of

Parliament David Lange and Mayor of Wellington Fran Wilde
to see if they would be trustees of the 'Wellington to Moruroa
Trust'. They agreed. These two figureheads would help us
lift the profile of the venture and establish credibility for
the fundraising effort. Local businessman Graeme Moore
and Phil Weeks, a marine broker, also agreed to become
trustees.

Nick Gales and I then met with Mr Fuimoano, a
Wellington solicitor of Samoan ancestry who was sympathetic
to the peace movement. 'Fui', as he was known, was a very
gentle and confident person and he agreed to help us with the
legal documents. He immediately dictated a couple of letters
to get us under way and planned to have the trust deed in
place by Monday morning to meet our campaign kick-off.

Our proposed sponsors required two conditions of the
trust:

1. If the three Wellington boats do not go to Moruroa,
then all monies used would be returned to the trust;

2. If the three Wellington boats do go to Moruroa, any
surplus funds would be donated to a non-political charitable
organisation.

With the makings of a trust in place, all we needed was
a bank account and people to put money in it. Through the
suggestion of Newstalk ZB, Westpac Bank, who was one of
their advertising clients, was willing to support the flotilla by
allowing donations to be made at their branches.

The popular Paul Holmes TV programme carried a
feature on the flotilla, focusing on the Auckland boats. It
appeared that the Auckland boats were finally getting their act
together. We thought time would tell. At this point there were
still only three confirmed boats going. Even we could not say
for sure that we were actually going, as the necessary funds
had not been raised.

Dennis and Nick gave a very positive live interview on
Wellington's new regional TV station Capital TV.

Janet Dalziell from Greenpeace called and informed us
that the large Greenpeace tug *MV Greenpeace* would be sailing
from Barcelona, Spain, to join the *Rainbow Warrior* at
Moruroa. Greenpeace was interested in co-ordinating the
communications for all yachts going, but would not be able to

contribute equipment or funds. I discussed with Janet the possibility of going inside the 12-mile Exclusion Zone at Moruroa. She said we would be able to meet with the Greenpeace skippers at Moruroa to discuss options.

Meanwhile, we were committed to putting *Joie* on the street in front of the French Embassy, but did not appreciate that it would be quite a fiasco to arrange, taking 3 days of full-time effort. The stunt involved a house moving trailer, a lifting crane, a boat cradle and heaps of bureaucracy in between.

Collins Cranes initially said they would do the lifting but then said they could only do it on Monday. Since we had already announced to the press that we were pulling the boat on Sunday, we were committed to that time. I then called the managing director of Titan Cranes, John Carter, who said he had heard me on the radio that morning and he agreed to help. Lew, the Maori driver of the crane, agreed to volunteer his time to the cause. I knew Lew personally. He was a fishing buddy of mine.

So it was arranged. Lew would pull us out of the water on Sunday and Collins Cranes would put us back in on Monday.

The next problem was arranging the truck and boat cradle. A number of calls were made for the truck and finally Britton House Movers agreed to help free of charge. They seemed to like what we were doing and knew the event would give them some advertising.

Organising the cradle turned out to be more of a nuisance. I called up the cruising club, where I was a member, and asked to borrow a cradle for a day. As it was mid-winter there were few people working on their boats and many cradles were available. They were strongly built ones, ideal for the job.

Although the commodore of the club initially said he thought it would not be a problem, later, after consulting other club committee members, he announced that they would not be able to loan us a cradle, citing the club's policy that no equipment was allowed off the premises. He said in the same breath, however, that they supported what we were doing.

At that point my temper raged, and I told him that they were not in support of what we were doing, or they would loan us a cradle. His answer was still NO! I hung up in disbelief.

Dennis, who was sitting next to me and overheard the conversation, was furious. "Give me his phone number," he asked. I said, "Settle down a little, count to 10 first." He said, "No, no, I'll be nice." He then called the club commodore and expressed his disbelief that they could not break some stupid committee rule to save the world. The answer was still NO!, although the commodore continued to say they were sympathetic to our cause.

I was completely embarrassed to be a member of such a club. They called themselves a Cruising Club. I hereafter nicknamed them the 'Abusing Club'! The South Pacific was their cruising ground, and yet they could not support a cause which 99 percent of New Zealand was behind, the removal of the French Government and their nuclear weapons from the region. Absurd! I vowed to resign from the club and did so on my return to New Zealand.

Plan B was to call Mike Muir Boat Builders. Mike put me on to Barbara Miller of Little Ship Supplies, who had a cradle, but it might require some welding to strengthen it. I inspected it. It was a rusty cradle, somewhat risky for what we were planning to do with it, but we would have to take a chance, as it was our last option. For a bottle of rum, the deal was done.

Other co-ordination involved Lambton Harbour Management, who allowed us to transport *Joie* by trailer along the Wellington waterfront property. It was possible to move *Joie* from the Taranaki Street Wharf, where she was to be lifted out of the water onto the trailer, along the waterfront property to the French Embassy, without having to go on the public road except for a very small stretch.

We had to arrange gate keys from Lambton Harbour Management and pick up parking meter cover bags from the Wellington City Council to reserve the space across the road from the Embassy.

At 3 p.m. on Sunday, 30 July, Titan Cranes and Britton Moving Company met me at Evan's Bay Yacht Club to pick up the cradle and secure it to the trailer. I left before them to move *Joie* around to Taranaki Street Wharf where they would meet us for the lift.

Paul McMaster, a fit young man who was later confirmed as crew for the trip, donned his wet-suit and jumped into the icy winter water to make sure the crane strap was properly placed around the hull, away from the propeller shaft and rudder.

Lew expertly lifted her out of the water and placed her perfectly in the cradle. Because it was a cradle of older design, it took us considerable time to adjust and pack out the cradle arms for transport. Jon, from *New Zealand Maid*, took charge and between myself, Paul McMaster, Dennis, and father and son moving team Graeme and Paul Britton, we managed to secure *Joie* on the cradle, much to the disgruntlement of three people whose cars we had unwarily blocked in the wharf.

One of these cars was a late model Mercedes Benz whose two occupants looked and dressed like the Mafia. The driver yelled abuse after abuse at us in a foreign accent, perhaps Italian I thought. He was virtually foaming at the mouth and I thought he might become violent. We had blocked them in for at least an hour.

They had been visiting a large freighter. My imagination began to work overtime. Perhaps they were in the middle of a drug smuggling operation, and we were holding them up from their rendezvous meeting. 'Oh hell, wouldn't that make the headlines,' I dreamed: 'MORUROA YACHTIES GUNNED DOWN BY DRUG SMUGGLING GANGSTERS!' I kept a close eye on them anyway.

When we were finally able to move the trailer to one side, they sped through the gap, as if on their way to a fire. As they passed they showed us the appropriate finger and the driver angrily cursed, 'this is a f*cking public wharf you bastards.' We held up our hands and shrugged to indicate our lack of control and innocence in the matter. I, however, whispered my own retaliatory phrase: 'arseholes!'

With *Joie* securely sitting high off the ground on the trailer, we planned to leave her on the Taranaki Street Wharf overnight and truck her around to the Embassy first thing in the morning before the rush hour traffic.

With the bottom covered in growth from sitting in the harbour for nearly a year, we all pitched in to scrub her down to make her a little more presentable for Chirac and the TV cameras. It was a difficult job as *Joie* was high up on the trailer, it was dark, and there was no water supply except the sea water in the harbour. Dennis and I scrubbed with long handled brooms while Cham Keel and Paul fetched bucket after bucket of water from the harbour using a long rope to reach the 10 feet from the wharf to the sea. They tossed the buckets of water at the hull, rinsing down our newly scrubbed areas as well as Dennis and me much of the time!

I slept high on *Joie* that night to protect her from any unexpected visitors. At 3 a.m. I got up to place signs on the wharf along the path we would be taking, to prevent people from parking in the way.

A police team were giving their police dogs an early morning practice run on the wharf. They looked suspiciously at me and no doubt wondered what I was up to so early in the morning. I walked over to them and explained myself after which they said, 'Good on you guys.' In fact, during the course of the protest we did not see one police officer, which seemed unusual as far as public protests go. The police were very supportive of what we were doing and stayed completely out of our way.

At daybreak, Graeme and Paul Britton arrived. While they hooked up the truck to the trailer, Dennis and I finished putting on the special signs we had made. They covered most of both sides of the boat and said: 'CHIRAC, WE ARE COMING'. On a pole we flew a large green flag with the peace symbol painted on it in white.

We began the move, and what an impressive sight it was. *Joie* was slowly moved towards the French Embassy, fully flagged in her protest garb. Capital TV came out early to film the move.

Graeme and Paul Britton were very experienced drivers and had the most amazing trailer. The whole bed of the trailer was on hydraulics and could be raised by 7 feet to clear the way above cars or other objects. The 24 wheels of the trailer also swivelled, so it could virtually go sideways if necessary. When we finally arrived at location they miraculously manoeuvred the trailer, with 13 tonnes of boat on it, sideways off the road, over the kerb, and onto the footpath of Frank Kitts Park.

VOILA! We did it! We were there, across from the French Embassy! Dennis and I couldn't actually believe we had pulled it off. We grinned in jubilation. We were exhausted. The cost of doing the stunt would normally have been thousands of dollars. We did it for $180 plus three cases of beer and a bottle of rum. That's cooking! And it was all possible because of the spirit and kind contributions of the moving and lifting people.

Two local musicians, Kevin and Mark, arrived to help us with the protest. They had written the wonderful Chirac Attack Song, which had a good jingle and great lyrics about Chirac and his French-minded persistence to explode nuclear bombs. It was so popular that radio station 2ZB played it constantly. Kevin and Mark announced they were going to donate proceeds from the sale of the song to the flotilla effort. They got up on top of *Joie* and started waving the large peace flag at oncoming traffic. Cars began honking like crazy in support of the protest. We estimated that over 10 000 cars honked that morning as they drove to work.

The Lindsay Yeo Breakfast Show began broadcasting at 6.30 a.m. from Chaffers Marina where *Kela* and *New Zealand Maid* were moored. Justin Du Fresne came down to *Joie* and began broadcasting live crossovers to Lindsay at the marina. Justin said from one of his live crossovers, "We are across the street from French territory, where the French could actually look out the window and see a protest yacht." 'Great stuff,' I thought. I also went on air live on two occasions and invited the French Embassy staff to come across the street and shake our hands and donate to the flotilla fund. They didn't!

The Newstalk ZB radio campaign kick-off was successful: an early morning sausage sizzle, espresso machine and live talkback. Mayor Fran Wilde, Nicky Hager and the other crew and skippers all took their turns on air. Even the skipper of the Greenpeace vessel *Rainbow Warrior*, who was in the South Pacific at the time, made an appearance on the radio show.

The advertisers then had their turn, and they got on the

air and announced their pledges to the flotilla: Moore Wilson donated $1,000 in food; Williams and Adams $500 cash; Hazelwood's $500 cash. A total of $4,000 was donated on the air. This was of course all pre-arranged by Newstalk ZB, but it made good radio. The managing directors of these popular local companies got on the air and said a few nice words in support of the cause before announcing their donations.

Dennis arranged a number of festivities at the protest site, including two 'French saboteurs' who emerged from Frank Kitts Park wearing wet-suits. They ran up to *Joie* and placed 'limpet' mines on the hull (tin pans with blue-tack). The audience bombarded the make-believe saboteurs with a liberal supply of water balloons.

At 12.30 p.m. that day, the protest ended. We moved *Joie* back to Taranaki Street Wharf and craned her back into the water. After motoring her back to her berth at Chaffers Marina, I directed the movers to Mike Muir boat builders where we dropped off the cradle. As they unloaded the cradle, I went down the road and bought a couple of cases of beer for them in appreciation of their contribution. They were great guys. I then went back to *Joie*, and went straight to bed. I was exhausted. Good day!

After the high of Monday, Tuesday turned out to be a bummer. All the work we put into the campaign kick-off appeared far from fruitful. All of the press releases, reporters and TV cameras resulted in far less coverage than we expected and needed. We made page three of the Evening Post and Dominion newspapers and only Channel 3 TV and Capital TV covered the story. The large national TV channels TV1 and TV2 did not cover the story at all. Unfortunately for us, that same day the police found and arrested the South Auckland serial rapist who had been terrorising residents for years. His capture made headline news in all the main papers.

Also, adding to our bummer day, we checked the flotilla trust bank account balance and discovered that Wellingtonians contributed only $345 to the Westpac account. This, plus the $4,000 Newstalk ZB clients donated, gave us a grand total of $4,345. Hardly the $75,000 we needed to raise.

Well, another meeting. We discussed alternatives:

1. Internet. We would be meeting with Peter Moon of Speakezy NZ Ltd regarding placing a web advertisement asking for donations.

2. Contacting all Wellington schools asking for their support and fund-raising.

3. Approach businesses directly for donations.

4. More focus on the street appeal.

Dennis was concerned that we hadn't enough people resource to help out sufficiently. Paul McMaster, Catherine Lockyer and Marianne Hardgraves were busy fundraising in the Wairarapa area and reported raising $350.

Ken Anderson, Dennis's friend and another fireman from Lower Hutt, came on board nearly full-time. They helped with the distribution of donation buckets to stores in the Wellington area. Ken arranged to get Thames Publications to print 150 posters in green to go along with the buckets at the sites. They did it free of charge.

August 6, 1995: Hiroshima Day, 50th anniversary
On 6 August, the first flotilla boats left for Moruroa. Before long we heard reports of storms and difficulties with rigging and electrics. The boats were: Barry Keon's *Triptych*, a 65-foot trimaran, carrying Television New Zealand crew and Inmarsat (telephone and facsimile capability at sea); *Photina*, a 38-foot Hershoff ketch out of Whitianga, skippered by John Simpson; *Aquila d'Oro*, a 52-foot yacht owned and skippered by prominent New Zealand lawyer Peter Williams; and the *R Tucker Thompson*, an 85-foot gaff-rigged topsail schooner, skippered by Russell Harris from the Bay of Islands. We heard that there were a few hundred people on the wharf at Opua to send *R Tucker Thompson* off.

It was an appropriate time for the first flotilla boats to leave for such a mission. On 6 August 1945, 50 years previously, a uranium bomb code-named 'Little Boy' was dropped on Hiroshima, killing 45 000 people instantly. Many of them were vaporised, leaving only their shadows behind. Many pregnancies resulted in miscarriage or stillbirth. Some 4.1 square miles of the city were completely destroyed. Delayed radiation effects including increased cancer rates put the final estimated death toll of the Hiroshima bomb at around 200 000. Three days later, on 9 August, a plutonium bomb code-named 'Fat Man' was exploded over Nagasaki. There were 22 000 immediate casualties, with an estimated final death toll of around 100 000 people.

To join in with the occasion we decided to have a Wellington flotilla commemoration ceremony on the water, with our three boats joined by five other supporting yachts, and many of our hard working supporters. We displayed banners saying 'CHIRAC WE'RE COMING', and 'STOP BOMBING MORUROA'. We motored slowly to the shore of nearby Frank Kitts Park where a land ceremony was taking place. All boats formed a circle. The crew said a few words before a wreath was cast into the sea in memory of the thousands of people who died in the bombing. We then motored northward near the shores of Oriental Parade and Evans Bay, displaying our banners. Many people came outside from their homes and waved to us in support. After the morning of exultation, we retired to the marina to our busy preparation schedules.

Later in the evening about 300 people took part in a ceremony at Frank Kitts Park Lagoon. They floated candle-lit lanterns carrying anti-nuclear messages in English and Japanese across the lagoon.

The issue of insurance for the flotilla vessels came up and the media took to it like a hungry dog to a bone; the media loves a controversy. The insurance industry decided they were not going to insure any of the flotilla yachts because the risk was too high. Their policies excluded cover for going into areas of 'war-like operations, civil war, mutiny or civil commotion'. They considered Moruroa a 'hostile zone'. An insurance broker was quoted as saying, 'it would only take one boat to go down, and all your profits would be gone.' Gee, what a nice thing to say. Here we were, three Wellington boats, and we were prepared to risk everything we had, including our lives, and these guys were worried whether they would make a profit or not.

The media made such a big deal out of it before even bothering to ask the flotilla boats if we wanted insurance. Most cruising yachts do not carry insurance because it is too expensive and adds nothing to the preparation of an ocean passage. The best insurance you could have is to put your money into good sound safety equipment, navigational aids and other supplies.

I had always been somewhat sceptical of certain aspects of the insurance industry. One way of looking at them is basically parasites feeding off the fear and risks of other people. Insurance companies often promote the delusion of a world full of crime, accidents and disease, then take your money to insure you against it. They will not play the game, though, unless the odds were stacked highly in their favour. As a result, they can afford to build the biggest and tallest buildings in the world, hire thousands of employees and make billions in profits.

Georgina Bailey from the Dominion newspaper phoned me asking for a Wellington position on the insurance issue. I stuck it to the insurance industry a little by saying, "They are in the business of insuring people against risk and they are not doing their job." The Government was asked to underwrite the flotilla but they refused, saying it was not their role.

The insurance industry eventually came to the party saying they would provide insurance coverage for half the value of the yachts. Mr Sargeant, chief executive of the Insurance Council, announced the 'generous concession' and said, "The business decision on whether to insure this trip or not was black and white and remains so. The moral decision is a different story. Council members are prepared to take this risk because they believe the flotilla will be making an important statement on nuclear testing on behalf of New Zealand, not because they believe it to be an insurable risk."

'Come on insurance people! I thought. 'The reason for the change of heart was that the insurance industry was exposed for just what they were; and it was not a pretty sight. Well, thanks for the half cover offer. But no thanks, we had more important things to spend our money on. Insurance was not even on our 'To Do' list.'

Dennis and Nick, who were very good at talking to the media, continued to do radio interviews and maintain a presence in the media. Consequently, fundraising improved. Ken Anderson, Dennis, John Warren, Cham Keel and Gunda successfully rallied collectors. We had around $10,000 in the kitty, though this was hardly enough to share between three boats. I had already committed over $10,000 in boat repairs for *Joie* alone and we had yet to put a dent in our 'To Do' list or provision the boat for the long journey.

CHAPTER 4

September 1995:
The World Reacts

I had never been involved in anything which had such strong international support. The international community seemed united in condemning the French Government's decision to resume testing, and this gave me strong resolve to press on with preparations to join the Moruroa flotilla.

Down-under, public opinion polls showed that 95 percent of New Zealanders were against French nuclear testing in the Pacific. In Australia, 96 percent opposed it. Some were dead serious, burning the French Consulate's office in Perth. Even in Chirac's own country, 60 percent of the French population opposed the resumption of testing, including former French President François Mitterrand and French Socialist leader Lionel Jospin, who publicly spoke out against the decision. M Jospin said that the planned tests were 'unnecessary and uncontrollable', and a 'pseudo-Gaullist gesture'. All around the world, governments, organisations and individuals reacted with horror and protested in any way that they could.

The Australian Government, chair country of the South Pacific Forum, quickly sent a delegation to Paris to meet the French Foreign Minister Hervé de Charette. The Forum considered an anti-testing publicity campaign in France, but the idea failed to gain sufficient support from other Forum members. Nevertheless, a limited campaign grew on its own, with open letters by Australian Prime Minister Paul Keating in *Le Monde* and an interview with Gareth Evans published in *Le Figaro*.

The delegation, which included representatives from

Nauru, Papua New Guinea and Western Samoa, had sought commitments that, after the test series was over, France would permanently close the test site and sign the South Pacific Nuclear-free Zone Treaty. The French Government's response was that no guarantees could be made on such matters until after a CTBT was signed.

Meanwhile, a group of New Zealand Members of Parliament representing all the major political parties presented a petition to French Ambassador Jacques Le Blanc in Wellington.

French Prime Minister Alain Juppé, not expecting such a hostile reaction from South Pacific countries, said his Government was ready to maintain medium- and long-term co-operation with all the countries of the region once 'this difficult period' had passed. The suspicion immediately arose that France would consider cutting aid to any South Pacific countries which took a hard line on French testing. Was it just coincidental that the French Government gave a 2200-tonne fuel tanker to the Tonga Government, who had adopted a conservative position on the issue of French testing in the South Pacific?

Meanwhile the situation began warming up with the arrival of the Greenpeace vessel *Rainbow Warrior* at Papeete. She was welcomed by a cheering crowd of 10 000 people, including pro-independence activists calling for a referendum on whether France should be allowed to resume nuclear testing in their islands. It was reported that French officials had tried to bar the *Rainbow Warrior* from entering Papeete's downtown port for 'security reasons', but thought better of it as the crowd swelled to 15 000.

The demonstrators blocked off roads into Papeete for a number of days, causing shortages of petrol and supermarket stocks. Oscar Temaru, leader of French Polynesia's main independence group, had at one stage said they would not lift the roadblocks until the authorities agreed to a referendum on the testing. He was told by French officials that it was impossible to hold such a referendum. The protest lasted 4 days before the French military gained control.

Greenpeace, realising the strong support it had from local French Polynesians, created a stunt that attracted massive publicity and acted as a catalyst for world-wide opposition to the planned tests: its crew sailed the *Rainbow Warrior* from Papeete directly to Moruroa and into the 12-mile Exclusion Zone.

After the customary number of warnings, the French frigate *Vendemiaire*, which until then had been following *Rainbow Warrior* at a distance, and the patrol ship *Railleuse*, closed in on them. *Rainbow Warrior* steamed at full speed straight for the atoll's entrance. The *Vendemiaire* launched a helicopter to over-fly *Rainbow Warrior*, and a Zodiac carrying about a dozen navy commandos with balaclavas and tear gas grenades around their belts came alongside. They threw a ladder onto the ship and climbed aboard. At the same time, a huge naval tug, the 4000-horsepower *Rari*, rammed the *Rainbow Warrior*, forcing her off course. The tug stayed in front of the ship, immobilising her.

The campaign's spokeswoman, New Zealander Stephanie Mills, shut herself in the radio room with a couple of other Greenpeace people and broadcast messages to the world. The world heard her screams as commandos eventually smashed the radio room portholes and tossed in tear gas grenades, gaining final control over the ship.

While commandos took over the ship, four inflatables with Greenpeace activists entered the lagoon and locked themselves to the drilling rig. When they were captured, all except Alice Richard Leney gave their name as Fernando Pereira, the Greenpeace photographer who was killed by French saboteurs in 1985 when they bombed the *Rainbow Warrior* in Auckland Harbour. Leney told the French authorities his name was Jeton Anjain, a senator from the Marshall Islands who had died of cancer the previous year. The senator had fought hard for the rights of his island people who were adversely affected by American nuclear weapons testing in the Marshalls during the 1950s.

The communications equipment on the *Rainbow Warrior* was state of the art, and its crew were actually able to videotape parts of the raid and beam out the pictures by satellite for the whole world to witness. This was obviously a significant factor in the French decision to release the *Rainbow Warrior* and its crew a day later in international waters without charge. People around the world denounced France for their use of violence and unreasonable force: the ramming and tear-gassing of the protest ship.

French officials privately acknowledged that the Government underestimated the diplomatic and commercial price France would pay, and the damage to its image by pictures of navy commandos tear-gassing Greenpeace activists on the *Rainbow Warrior*.

In the European Parliament, Jacques Chirac was actually booed and heckled by dozens of members and one speaker dubbed him a 'neo-Gaullist Rambo'. Several other leaders also joined in denouncing the tests. Chancellor Kohl, France's closest European ally, aware of a poll showing 95 percent of Germans opposed the testing, registered his dissent; Italian President Oscar Luigi Scalfaro asked him to reconsider; Dutch Prime Minister Wim Kok told him the tests were 'undesirable'; and Sweden's political parties were encouraging a boycott of French goods.

By now, the countries where boycotts had been called for accounted for 40 percent of France's export sales of wines and spirits, worth $11 billion a year.

Chirac's first major decision as President had put him offside with his allies, made France the target of protest around the world and exposed French products to consumer boycotts. Was his decision on the tests still 'irrevocable'?

In reaction to all the negative publicity and pressure from Greenpeace, the French Government stepped up their own public relations campaign. French Polynesian President Gaston Flosse and other government officials loyal to the French Government went on a fishing trip to Moruroa. Of course, they were accompanied by an entourage of French journalists. The 3-day trip included a swim in the lagoon, diving for lobster, fishing and a seafood barbecue.

The French Government also invited journalists from all over the world to visit Moruroa. Many came, more than 30 in one weekend alone from France and Germany, with another 40 from other parts of Europe and the Asia Pacific region. They also invited the American news media. At these briefings, General Paul Vericel, director of France's nuclear weapons test site at Moruroa, warned reporters that he would take 'all necessary means' to ensure no protest flotilla boat breached the 12-nautical mile restricted area during the tests. "France's sovereignty will be enforced," he said.

A second wave of anti-French reaction was gathering force. Japan decided to table a resolution in August in the UN against French testing and the Russian Parliament condemned France's move. France recalled its ambassador from Australia for consultations after Australian Defence Minister Robert Ray barred Dassault Aviation from bidding for a A$740 million contract to supply jet fighters. The French Government also accused the Australians of a series of other 'hostile' gestures, including stopping mail to the French Embassy, delaying diplomatic bags twice, allowing demonstrators to obstruct access to the French Embassy and delaying French ships in Australian ports. The French Government announced it was reviewing coal and uranium contracts with Australian firms worth A$260 million.

The Australians were an obvious target for a problem that got too big for the French Government. Adding to the pressure was the sentiment expressed at the Association of South-East Asian Nations Foreign Ministers meeting, which was highly against France, including strong reactions from Japan and Indonesia. But still the French Government would not back down. French Prime Minister Alain Juppé again declared that France would stand firm.

By now, more than 150 states and millions of people around the world condemned France for its plans. The French Government was starting to buckle a little under this enormous international pressure. They began dropping hints that they may not need to conduct all eight tests; that they would allow independent scientists and European Union experts to inspect Moruroa after the testing; and that after the tests, they would propose that the Comprehensive Test Ban Treaty become truly comprehensive! France's ambassador to the Geneva Disarmament Conference, Gerard Errera, said that France would put up a proposal ensuring the treaty 'prohibit any nuclear weapon test explosion or any other nuclear explosion', including low-yield blasts. Previously, France had reserved the right to continue small-scale tests indefinitely.

Protests mounted against the resumption of French

nuclear testing:

- The largest ever anti-nuclear march took place in Rarotonga, Cook Islands, led by the Prime Minister Sir Geoffrey Henry, and included a quarter of the city's population.
- 2500 people marched on the French Embassy in Fiji's capital, Suva.
- South Pacific Islands countries announced that France was no longer welcome in the Pacific and they labelled the testing as a 'malicious and systematic' destruction of their environment.
- Australia: French Embassy in Perth burnt; maritime workers refused French Government ships entry into Australian ports; 10 000 people in Sydney marched on the French Consulate.
- The New Zealand Council of Trade Unions urged unions in New Zealand and throughout the Pacific to join forces to ban trade with France and 5000 letters of complaint were delivered to the French Embassy in New Zealand.
- The 19-member Association of South-East Asian Nations called for an immediate halt to nuclear testing.
- In France, 400 scientists rejected as 'an insult' the Government's justification for the tests and, in Paris, more than 3000 people demonstrated against the tests.
- Protests took place in several other European capitals, including Copenhagen, London, Luxembourg, Dublin and Berne, where a French train was also firebombed.
- The European Parliament condemned the tests and voted 331–74 to urge France and other nuclear powers to sign a test ban treaty by the end of the following year.

Probably the most bizarre of the protests came from the Australian sex industry lobby group Eros Foundation. They announced that "in the spirit of the great epithet, make love not war", they would boycott French knickers, French letters,

French kisses and French sex. President Fiona Patten said the Australian industry bought A$250,000 of erotic products from France each year. She also said, "The industry is also undertaking a major review of language and terminology within the sex industry which paints the French as lovers and therefore peaceful."

CHAPTER 5

Underway to Moruroa

The New Zealand Government finally conceded to growing public pressure to provide more support for the flotilla and announced that it would be sending a ship to monitor the tests. On August 13, we had a briefing on *Kela* by Commander and Assistant Chief of Naval Staff (Operations), Bill Rathburn. He was very professional and supportive of what we were doing, but informed us that *Tui*, the government unarmed oceanographic research vessel that would be going to Moruroa, would only be able to provide emergency assistance outside the 12-mile Exclusion Zone around Moruroa. If any of the flotilla vessels 'went in' and were in 'hot pursuit' by the French military, they could not assist us, even if we came back outside the 12-mile zone. He further advised that, if we should go into the zone, they were required to warn us and request us to come back out again.

The *Tui* would not supply any provisions or assist in communications unless in an emergency. They were not even allowed to make radio contact with the Greenpeace boats. They could not, for political reasons, be seen as supporting the protest flotilla. 'Why are we even having this meeting? There is nothing here for us,' I thought to myself at the time. Really, what Bill Rathburn insinuated was that there was nothing much they could do for us. We walked away from the meeting aghast.

Two members of Parliament would be joining *Tui*. They were Brian Neeson from National and Chris Carter from Labour. With Neeson in Government and Carter in the Opposition, I wondered how they would get along for such a long time at sea on the same boat. Chris Carter was obviously very keen. He revealed plans earlier to take a dinghy into

Moruroa. The idea was promptly squashed by Prime Minister Jim Bolger and Labour leader Helen Clark.

On 14 August, with Dennis fully in charge of fundraising activities, I concentrated on getting *Joie* ready. Earlier, I had removed the mast and begun a major fit-out, which included the checking of all rigging, installation of new electrical wires, mast navigational lights, halyards and halyard winches. I now made a list of other necessary jobs and equipment needed. It seemed like a massive list. Could I really do this all in just over one week? I did not even bother calculating how much it would all cost. I knew it would be too much, much more than I could afford. Jon and Nick were both in the same predicament. Their lists were just as long, if not longer. Our marina pier looked like a huge 'working bee' day and night.

Joie To Do List

Work Items and Repairs
- Re-build front hatch and re-rubber seal
- Build storage lockers in engine room
- Re-build aft cabin companionway hatch
- Install galley bilge pump
- Seal top of fuel tank
- Re-weld broken bow roller
- Make and install anchor chain hole cover plate
- Install new head portlight
- Re-seal four existing portlights
- Install latches on all hatches
- New door and seal on forward bulkhead
- Repair broken stanchion
- Sew new bunk lee cloths and install them

- Install four eye bolts for dinghy tie-down
- Screw down floor boards
- Make latches for bunk seat compartments
- Haul out boat for:
  - Propeller shaft flange re-fit
  - New seal & re-pack propeller shaft gland
  - Design and install rudder post seal
  - Two new sea cocks
  - Anti-foul hull
  - New zincs

Rigging and sailing gear
- Check all rigging
- Install two new halyard winches
- Change halyards to internal wire/rope halyards

- New mast wiring
- Install wind direction vane
- Paint mast and boom
- Repair No. 2 and Storm sails
- Sail repair kit (cloth, strapping, needles, twine)
- Fix boom traveller
- Grease all winches

Engine
- Install new 55 amp alternator
- Install three new batteries
- Install new three-way voltage regulator
- Change engine oil

Electronic / Electrical
- Rewire fuse holders
- Build fuse box weather protector
- Replace battery cables
- New search light
- Install Single Side Band radio
- Install new VHF radio
- New navigational lights for mast

Safety Equipment
- Install new EPRIB (emergency positioning device)
- Obtain four safety harnesses
- Man overboard pole and light
- Two man overboard horseshoe buoys with drogues
- First Aid Kit, and current drugs
- Set of distress signals
- Re-service 6-man life-raft
- Install external emergency manual bilge pump
- Install three new fire extinguishers
- Install new upper and lower life lines
- Large U-bolts for emergency rudder
- Heaving line for man-overboard
- Tie on wooden safety plugs to all sea-cocks
- Two new wire jack-stays for attaching safety harnesses

Navigation
- Install new GPS monitor and antenna
- Obtain current:
    Light Lists for S Pacific/NZ
    Nautical Almanac for sight reductions
    Charts for S Pacific Islands

Other Equipment & Things to do
- Buy foul weather gear for crew
- Inflatable dinghy & oars
- Obtain extra LPG bottle
- Get a selection of tools, including hacksaw blades
- Sit test for radio operator's license

New Zealand Maid went back into the water after completing her underwater work and *Kela* went up in her place. There was only one haul-out slip in the marina. I was suppose to go up the next day, but heard from Nick that having spent $500 for a shaft packing gland, it didn't fit right. That was the normal story for yachts. It's not quite like buying a part for your car. Nick was delayed for another day.

By the end of the day we knocked a few items off of the 'To Do' list. The emergency manual bilge pump got installed with a three-way switch to pump either from the main cabin or engine room. We also managed to get the rest of the portlights caulked, the SSB radio fully installed and the GPS monitor mounted.

I finally confirmed the crew for *Joie*. Dennis, who initially said he would not be able to go, showed up one day waving a piece of paper in his hand and smirking sheepishly. I ask him what it was. He said, "This is my resignation from the Fire Service. Do you want a crew to Moruroa?" I said, "Far out, you're on." I did not even give it a second thought, though I learned later from Nicky Hager that Dennis was sacrificing a large redundancy payment from the Fire Service by resigning early.

Dennis said, "I am very disappointed that the line in New Zealand seems to be, 'Oh well, we're all going to go up there and we're going to have a peaceful protest'; no one is ever going to cross the line and we are just going to sit around outside the thing. Oh hell! That's not for me." I said, "I agree with you Dennis, they're all a bunch of pansies, aren't they? Well I tell you, if *Joie* is going all that way, we'll be looking at doing a little more than just sitting around on our butts." With that, Dennis seemed content to join the *Joie* crew.

Paul McMaster and Paul Giles, both of whom had sailed with me in the past, were also confirmed as crew. So we had four blokes going to Moruroa. We were in a different situation than *Kela* and *New Zealand Maid*, who would be taking their young families with them.

I was frustrated and disappointed with the amount of time my confirmed crew were putting into getting *Joie* ready for sea. It seemed like an insurmountable task and I had been readying the boat mostly on my own. Dennis, however, was tied up with the campaign fund-raising, and the two Pauls were busy trying to sort out their jobs and family commitments.

In my left hand, I held up the boat 'To Do' list and, with my right hand, I could count the days to go before blast-off. It did not take me long to realise that we weren't going to make it unless there was more help.

Dennis came to the rescue and recruited more firemen friends. John Curtis, Hugh Parsons, Dave Wright, John Reeve, Ken Anderson and Ken Sanders all came down and offered their services. I moved into a delegating and organising role. These guys worked like they were putting out a fire, and things started coming together very fast.

John Curtis single-handedly anti-fouled the boat. Ken Anderson and Ken Sanders took over the electrics, re-wiring and replacing fuse holders. The latches got installed, the pumps got installed. Scott Feasey came down and helped with the building work, which included the engine room stowage and hatches. The place was a hive of activity.

Young Paul finally sorted out his affairs, and arrived eager to go. He was a fireball of energy and loved the 'To Do' list. He carried it around with him, often stuffing it into his pocket, like some people do with dollar bills. He got great satisfaction with crossing off items as they were completed. He crossed them off with such fury that one could not recognise the job which was completed. He often holed the paper in his 'job finished' ceremony.

The *Joie* 'To Do' list became a tattered, wrinkled, worn-out, stained, delicate and illegible piece of rag. Paul always wanted to review the list with me, but because of its state, we continually debated what had been completed and what the remaining 'to do' items were.

I decided to make a new list. A fresh list. But this time I would not let Paul touch it! Paul was frustrated by this so he transferred items from my list to his own, then proceeded to destroy his in the course of a day's work. At the end of the day we would compare my fresh list with his tattered one to judge the progress made.

Although Giles could not put in as much time because of job commitments, he was invaluable in organising much of the safety and other equipment, including an EPRIB, safety harnesses, rubber dinghy, VHF radio, lee cloths, fire extinguishers and other gear. He also repaired the bow roller and caulked and sealed all the portlights.

Rozellia Mawhinney took over the responsibility for provisions, the first aid kit, and organising discounts with suppliers for equipment such as foul weather gear. She also volunteered to look after the Wellington Peace Flotilla office while we were away. She was really great, and it was good to know someone would be continuing with the media work, communications, fund-raising and other jobs while we were at sea.

Both *Kela* and *New Zealand Maid* had finalised their crew lists. John Wilson and Quentin Hanich, from Melbourne, Australia and Diarmuid Brazendale and Marty Skelton from Wellington, would join the *Kela* family. That gave them a crew of eight people. On *New Zealand Maid*, in addition to their family of five, Adriaan Stroess and Jim MacArthur joined the crew. Adriaan was an experienced square rigger sailor, and Jim was a diver who worked on a past Greenpeace drift-net campaign.

Chimera, a 55-foot Robert's sloop, which had also joined the Peace Flotilla, arrived in Wellington from Greymouth, a small town on the west coast of New Zealand's South Island. The skipper, Gary Shearer, and his two other crew, Reggie and Des, were a tough lot, and reminded me of cowboys ready to take on the wild west. None of them had any ocean going experience. They were to take on two more crew from Auckland: Daniel Salmon and Martin Taylor. These two were university students who were doing a video documentary about the Moruroa Peace Flotilla for their film class. *Chimera* would be leaving with us from Wellington on 23 August. It was great to have another boat going along.

It was encouraging to see that the Government had filed its application with the World Court in The Hague asking for an urgent hearing on the proposed French tests. They would be attempting to reopen New Zealand's 1973 World Court case that argued that the environmental threat posed by nuclear testing contravened international law. MP Paul East, who headed the legal team, maintained that France should carry out a full environmental impact assessment on Moruroa and Fangataufa atolls before any tests were carried out. Other nations had joined in support of the New Zealand case including Australia, Western Samoa, the Solomons, the Marshall Islands and the Federated States of Micronesia.

A number of legal experts had already commented that the case was 'a long-shot'. One reason was that France no longer accepted the jurisdiction of the World Court. This was a difficult argument to contend with. The other point was that since the tests had been moved underground it was difficult to prove that there was or had been any environmental impact. Adding to the difficulty was that New Zealand's own nuclear radiation expert, Andrew MacEwan, had been publicly quoted as saying the environmental risks of French testing were negligible.

To me, although the environmental aspects of the testing had to be questioned, they were not the main issue. The real issue was that France was taking the nuclear arms race a step forward. They made a mockery of the Comprehensive Test Ban Treaty by pushing their technology ahead to the point where everybody else had to catch up. For the sake of the human race, it must be opposed at all costs.

August 23, 1995
WE DID IT!! We were under way. There was a great farewell for us at Chaffers Marina. Many people showed up to bid us good luck and goodbye. It was awkward and stressful as friends and family were clambering all over the yachts, wanting to talk to us, while we were frantically trying to finish our last-minute provisioning and stowage, and getting departure clearance.

Kim McMoran came down amongst the crowd to give us our safety checks. We passed with flying colours. He was very thorough and took down the details of our life-raft, EPRIB, flares and fire extinguishers. He checked our safety harnesses, life raft, radios, charts, first-aid kit and other gear. On three occasions, he had to ask well-wishers who came aboard to leave the yacht so that he could finish his inspection. It was total chaos.

Then came New Zealand Customs with their Ten

Minute and other forms to fill out. Soon the clearance formalities were done, and we could leave the country. What a weird feeling that was.

Mayor Fran Wilde came to the occasion and gave a goodbye speech to the crowd, which was 400 strong. She said she was proud the flotilla was taking the message to Moruroa that nuclear testing was unacceptable to New Zealanders. She then presented us with Windsor the Gnome as a representative of the Mayor's office. She also gave us Absolutely Positively Wellington flags and hats for our boats and crew, and a $500 cheque (Dennis actually asked for $15,000!). Dennis interjected, 'The money had already been spent!' He then gave his off-the-cuff speech saying it was one of the hardest things he had ever done in all his life. He praised the spirit of the skippers and crew who were determined to do this thing at all costs, whether they raised enough finance or not. It was this spirit and determination, which he said was shared by nearly every New Zealander, that made him become involved and committed to the cause.

Jon Tucker also said a few words to the crowd. "The plan to go to Moruroa had been just an idea 5 weeks ago, but after a lot of sleepless nights and support from so many people we are actually going. I can't believe it! There had been a few moments when I doubted the wisdom of the trip, but it feels pretty neat to be going."

We motored to the fuel wharf, fuelled up, paid our bills to Barton Marine, Duffy the yacht rigger and others, and said our last goodbyes. There were lots of hugs, kisses and tears. Then we were off!

As we pulled out of the harbour, *Joie* was met by Paul Gubb on his charter boat *Sweet Georgia*. He had a Television New Zealand camera crew and other reporters on board. As they motored close to us, Dennis, the two Pauls and I lined up together on the port side of *Joie* and sang the Chirac Attack song to them. With our fists in the air we sang the only lyrics to the song we could remember: 'NO NUKES, NO NUKES, NO NUKES. WE DON'T WANT YOUR BOMB. CHIRAC ATTACK.' We sang this over and over again to the pleasure and approval of the camera men. The same camera crew filmed earlier that week at McGill's Tavern in Wellington where the song writers and flotilla participants performed for them. We guessed that they would be putting the whole story together for that evening's Holmes Show programme. 'Well, we won't be around to see that one!,' I thought.

Kela, New Zealand Maid and *Chimera* decided to stop in at Seaview Marina in Wellington Harbour overnight to finish last-minute stowing. They were obviously relieved to be out of Chaffers Marina and away from the press and crowds, but needed to tidy things up a little more before heading to sea. We were unaware that they had done this and we continued out through the heads of Wellington Harbour. Jon told me later that they had tried to call us on the VHF radio but could not get us on the likely channels.

As we beat out of the harbour against a 20-knot southerly, it suddenly became very quiet and relaxing. It was a wonderful feeling, as if someone had taken a huge weight off our shoulders. No more reporters asking questions, no more faxes to send, no more 'To Do' items to cross off. The four of us were high on our achievements. We did it, we were under way! It was the most amazing and wonderful feeling. We were going to Moruroa. We gave each other hugs and we screamed with joy into the wind at the top of our lungs. I grabbed a few beers from the galley and we drank them in celebration as we headed through the heads of Wellington Harbour.

Our jubilation did not last long as we soon came to the realisation that we had a whole set of new obstacles ahead of us: getting safely to Moruroa, which was around 3000 nautical miles to the north-east of us. As we left the heads and beat into a 2-metre swell, young Paul was first to christen our passage. He spewed and gagged repeatedly into the ocean. Giles soon joined him, then even I had a go. I had had nothing to eat all day and the motion of the boat combined with the beer had its way with me! Dennis was the only one not to join us. I noticed later he was clever enough, in all the commotion, to think of putting sea-sickness patches behind his ears.

We had a good sail for about 2 hours, as we made our way into Cook Strait. Then the southerly died out completely and we were becalmed until 3 a.m., when the wind began to build from the north-west. As the wind continued to freshen, I noticed that the gooseneck on the boom had slipped up over the mast boom track. The boom had completely disconnected from the mast and was only being held by the strength of the sail-cloth. I called Giles out of his bunk and, in the dark and wallowing sea, we dropped the main sail and put the heavy boom back on its track. When the boom came off, it had damaged a few sail slides and a section of sail track, which we semi-repaired the next morning. Little did we appreciate that this would only be the beginning of mishaps to plague us as we headed east.

They say it's not possible to leave New Zealand, particularly the southern half, without feeling the full force of Mother Nature. We did not expect the trip to Moruroa to be an easy one, at least for the first 3 weeks of the passage. We were departing Wellington in the middle of winter, and we would need to stay at around 40° S latitude for about 2 weeks to get our easting. This is a rough part of the world's oceans referred to in shipping and yachting circles as the 'Roaring Forties'. It is an area of sea which is uninterrupted by land except for the small country of New Zealand, and the southern tip of the continent of South America. And because of this expanse of open ocean, the wind and sea often build to great strength and height.

I sensed a bit of nervousness amongst my crew. Only Dennis had had some limited offshore experience before. It was really a strange and insecure feeling to be sailing away from our home city; to see it sink away over the horizon and to be replaced with the sea, a seemingly endless ocean as far as one could see. The feeling was intensified by not knowing what was in store for us. Would we run into a severe storm and drown? Would the boat hit a ship, whale or floating shipping container and instantly sink? Would someone accidentally fall overboard? Would the mast or rudder break, forcing us to drift aimlessly at sea until we perished?

The ocean is a vast place and when you are in it in a small boat you begin to feel insignificant; like a needle in a haystack. You start to question life and what it is all about. You are at the whim of the all-powerful ocean. You feel helpless and isolated. You are leaving behind everything that makes you feel comfortable: a warm home, your job, your car, friends, family, pets, and modern conveniences. If you are hungry you can no longer run down to the local takeaway. If you are thirsty you can't go to the pub. If you are sick you can't go to the doctor. If you are bored you can't go for a walk, or to a party, or to the rugby. You are now stuck on a cold and wet 42-foot 'surfboard' for an indefinite period of time with three other blokes you hardly know!

Despite the insecurity, we made very good easting under a 30-knot north-easterly, sailing better than 7 knots. 'Aries', our self steering vane, was doing a wonderful job on the helm and the GPS was just fantastic. At a touch of a button I could get an exact position, speed, course and distance to our destination. The GPS indicated that we were at 41° 50' S latitude. We would stay near 40° S latitude for the next 1920 nautical miles until we reached 140° W longitude. This would assure us ample westerly winds. Once we got to 140° W, we would head north into the south-easterlies, and the warm waters of the South Pacific.

Young Paul continued to be very seasick and was puking green bile, but he was still smiling. I gave him a suppository of phenegren to help him get over his sickness. We had a few laughs over this. We asked if we could watch him administer the medication. He denied us the opportunity and when he discreetly slid it in he said, "OK baby!"

We had our first 'sked' (short for scheduled radio contact) with *Kela* and *New Zealand Maid*. They and *Chimera* were about 60 nautical miles behind us. They motored out of the harbour at first light in calm conditions. Jon also informed me about the sked with the other Auckland boats and Greenpeace's *Rainbow Warrior* at 16.00 hours each day.

Giles, who had been listening to his Walkman in his bunk, said that the top news item was that Warren Cooper, the Minister of Foreign Affairs, announced that if any flotilla boats were to break the 12-mile limit and make their way to the *Tui*, she would be required to contact Parliament and not to release the crew to the French military. Parliament would decide whether or not to release the 'law breakers'. It sounded as if the Government had toughened up its stance a little with regard to the protest.

August 23

We passed the 180° parallel (international date line) and instantly lost one day! Great sailing; it was blowing about 35 knots with 3–4-metre swells. Crossing the date line must have been a jinx; we were soon victim of a series of mishaps. Firstly, the tang which holds the mainsheet onto the boom detached. The boom flew out to leeward, completely out of control, and fluttered in the wind. We had to drop the sail, in rather rough conditions, to repair it. We took the opportunity to rig a boom vang, which we had not done in part because of lack of time. We got under way again and made very good time.

Our GPS showed we were going up to 14 knots at times as we surfed down waves. When departing Wellington we had forgotten to clean out the cockpit drains and ended up with a lot of water in the engine room bilge. This spilled over into the sump, and out again, coating the engine room with a film of oil. No one volunteered to clean up in these sea conditions, so we decided to postpone this unpleasant task until the strong westerly eased.

Then, a main cabin portlight started leaking badly even though we re-rubbered it before leaving. Dennis went on deck and held a piece of plastic board over the hole from the outside, while Giles and I opened it on the inside, dried it out to the best of our ability, then prepared to caulk it. Dennis was unable to keep the water out and litres gushed in at one point. In the rolling seas we smeared the sealant all over the place then shut the portlight. It worked! No more leak.

We decided to fire up the diesel stove to get some warmth. This involved attaching a 5-foot section of stove stack to the deck chimney flange. In those seas, every small task was dangerous and not very easily accomplished.

Dennis crawled along the windward deck on his knees, clutching the stove stack between his arm and body, and holding on for dear life at the same time. He attached it and, when I fired up the stove, the heat was most welcome; we were all wet and cold. As evening rolled in we assessed the weather and decided to drop the double-reefed main and sail with only the small number 3 jib. Dropping the mainsail removed the low pressure area which had previously drawn the smoke out of the stove. As a consequence, the stove backwinded and diesel smoke billowed into the main cabin until the room was entirely filled.

Young Paul, still seasick, came clambering and coughing out of the smoke screen and onto the deck, gasping for fresh air. He was not very happy. The smoke gushed out of the main cabin for nearly 15 minutes before the diesel remaining in the burner was exhausted. Back to a cold, wet boat.

To top things off, *Joie* fell off a huge wave and many of the things in the hanging food storage net were strewn around the cabin; carrots, bread, crackers and onions were rolling around all over the floor.

As darkness fell, we hoped we were far enough away from the jinx date line to do us no further harm. Interestingly, that evening we could see many long tube-like objects floating on the water that glowed with phosphorescence, about the size of large cucumbers. What were these things? In all my sea travels, I had never seen these before. Were they an omen of some sort? Or were they just strange-shaped glowing jelly fish, unique to the Roaring Forties?

Dennis and I sat on deck in the cold darkness to ponder the day's events, only to be dowsed by a very large sea. Dennis remarked that he would never do this again. "I am cold, wet and tired; every little move is so strenuous and has to be calculated and planned," he said. I encouraged him that these were early days and he would get used to it.

We spoke to Jon on *New Zealand Maid*. They were about 100 nautical miles south-west of us and *Kela* was about 40 nautical miles behind them. *Sudden Laughter*, a Nelson-based catamaran, made radio contact. They were also en route to Moruroa, having left Picton in the South Island about the same time we left Wellington. Being a catamaran, we expected they would be a bit faster and begin closing the gap.

We were sailing with only the small number 3 jib and still making 7 knots. Good sailing!

August 24
We chalked up 200 nautical miles the previous day. Fast sailing with a 35–40-knot westerly wind off our quarter. We put up a double-reefed mainsail to assist the number 3 jib. This improved the motion and stability of *Joie*.

The wind shifted to south-west at 03.00 and I got up to give Dennis a hand with the course change. We jibed the main and adjusted 'Aries' and were soon on course again.

The night crew reported that a strange fish landed on the boat in the early hours of the morning. It was described as having tentacles like a squid, but with a fish head! "Why didn't you keep it?" I asked. "It could have been an unknown fish; we could have taken a picture of it." Dennis said, "It would have died, so we had to throw it back."

It did not look as if we had completely shaken off the date-line jinx, but some elements of good fortune were creeping in. That day a shackle came undone and the boom topping lift line separated from the boom. An amazing 'Act of God' saved the day. I was looking out of the main cabin companionway while Dennis was sitting in the corner of the cockpit. Out of the sky a heavy-duty shackle flopped directly into Dennis's lap. This was the same topping lift shackle which had come undone.

With an expression of surprise, he said, "someone's throwing things at me! Where the hell did this come from?" The pin to the shackle was rolling on the deck and Dennis quickly recovered it. The odds of something like that occurring in a 30-knot wind with a mixed sea and the boom far to leeward was simply unbelievable. It was a bit like winning Lotto.

We had our $25 shackle back in full, and started planning to get the topping lift line back into position from its state flying high from the mast top like a squirming snake. Dennis went forward. I disconnected Aries and we did a few '360s' in the ocean until Dennis miraculously caught it. We then dropped the sail, pulled the boom in and re-attached it. The total exercise took about an hour. We were exhausted, but under way again.

I asked young Paul to go down in the engine room to get the onions which were stored there. Unfortunately, they fell in the bilge and were covered with oil. Paul passed them up one by one, gagging all the time as if to have another puke. He was brave but resolved never to go down there again to smell the diesel fuel sloshing around in the bilge water in a rolling sea. We salvaged the onions by washing them in soapy

Picture taken shortly after deciding to go to Moruroa. The Wellington crew at that stage was, from left to right, Matthew, Barbara and Sam Tucker, Lynn Pistoll, Cath and Nick Gales with baby Jemma, and John Tucker. Photo by The Evening Post.

Paul McMaster on the Joie *outside the French Embassy. A dry run, but we were the first flotilla boat to reach French Territory! Photo by* The Evening Post.

Taking on fuel and stowing last minute items at Chaffers Marina shortly before leaving for the long trek to Moruroa. Photo by The Evening Post.

Our spirits lifted as we had our first nice day sailing since leaving Wellington. Left to right: Paul Giles, Paul McMaster with guitar (he only knew one song) and Dennis.

The Guinevere and crew just arriving at Moruroa after a 22-day sail from New Zealand. They were stationed for 9 days at Moruroa.

The R Tucker Thompson *under full sail: an 85-foot gaff-rigged square-topsail schooner skippered by Russell Harris from the Bay of Islands. We had many strategy meetings on this boat because she was the largest of the NZ Peace Flotilla.*

Arrival at Moruroa! The Kela just in front of us, taking on water and fuel by hose from the Tui after the 19 day passage. We were all surprised and pleased that the Tui's role had become more supportive of the flotilla than we had been told before leaving Wellington.

The French arriving by Zodiac to deliver two letters to us from the Admiral. He wrote that he respected our right to protest but if we went into the zone our vessels would be confiscated and our crew subjected to 'French discipline'.

The New Zealand Maid *puts on protest banners upon arrival at Moruroa.*

Helicopters were the best way for the French to photograph the crew to identify who was on board each vessel. They did this on a regular basis, causing a disturbance and mayhem on the smaller vessels with their down-draft.

The 38-foot ketch Vega *is being loaded with supplies and 19 Polynesians from the local islands of Tureia and Vanavana. They were sailing to Moruroa to claim their nuclear-contaminated island back from the French, who took it from them in 1963 without lease or deed of title.*

'Vicious protesters' meeting on Manutea. *The French probably hated them all! From left to right: Michelle Seather (Greenpeace activist), Audrey Cardwell (Greenpeace campaign co-ordinator), Sanae Shida (Executive Director of Greenpeace Japan), Chris Robinson (Greenpeace activist,* Vega*), Brad Ives (skipper,* Manutea*) and partner, Con Flinn (crew,* Photina*), David McTaggart (Honorary Chairman of Greenpeace), Alex (Greenpeace radio operator), Charlie (first mate,* Manutea*), Martin Taylor (flotilla crew) and John Simpson (skipper,* Photina*).*

water and taking off the outer skins. I cooked a nice stew from fresh vegetables and mince. With some real food in the crew's guts, they started to come alive.

It was a really good sked from the Greenpeace vessel *Rainbow Warrior* that evening. They were near Moruroa, and radioed all the yachts in the flotilla. The radio operator was unable to receive me because of *Joie's* small 35-watt transmitter, so I passed on our position and well-being to *New Zealand Maid*, who relayed it.

An unidentified person came on the air and announced to the flotilla that he had met a prominent French journalist. The journalist told him that his contacts in the French military had said that the French army were under instruction to remove any of the flotilla boats that went into the 12-mile Exclusion Zone. They were not to harm vessel or crew, but only to board and take them back outside the zone. This was very interesting and useful information. I hoped it was true!

Greenpeace signed off with a weather forecast. It was 19.00 hours and we were moving along at 7.5 knots with a fresh south-westerly blowing. I would make our scheduled call with *Kela* and *New Zealand Maid* at 20.00 hours.

Sked 20.00 hours. *New Zealand Maid* reported a problem getting their engine going. They had water down the exhaust manifold and into the engine. They were unable to charge their house batteries to operate the radio for prolonged transmissions. They were working on the situation and would report back at 06.45 hours. They would have to remove the injectors, then turn the engine over to push out the water. I did not envy them doing that in the bad sea conditions. It made me want to puke just thinking about it.

	Joie	*Kela*
Latitude S	40° 57'	40° 06'
Longitude W	175° 15'	177° 59'

Having a moment to myself, I sat down and read about how the French conducted their underground nuclear explosions at Moruroa and Fangataufa atolls. The vertical structure of each atoll consisted essentially of two rock sequences: a volcanic basalt basement and, capping it, sedimentary carbonate formations hundreds of metres thick. The carbonate formations are fairly porous and the basalt basements are of lower permeability, but all are saturated with sea water. There is slow migration of water from the ocean inwards, rising through the basalt basements and carbonate formations towards the lagoons.

Exploding a nuclear bomb there was quite a sophisticated process that involved drilling a 2-metre hole some 500–1200 metres deep into the extinct volcano. They drill down until they get into the hard basalt layer of the volcano. The bigger the bomb, the deeper they go. It takes between 4 and 8 weeks just to dig each hole. The bomb is then lowered into the shaft inside a 20-metre-long canister containing instruments that report on the first milliseconds of the explosion. The hole is then back-filled and plugged with tons of concrete.

At the time of detonation, the placid waters of the lagoon turn completely white, then foam and boil as venting from the explosion takes place. Observers have said that the shock waves kill fish in the lagoon and that the whole atoll sinks slightly with each nuclear explosion.

Underground, the explosion creates a large cavity in the volcanic rock. Temperatures are so high the rock vaporises, causing vitrification and glass formation. French officials claim this vitrified cavity, or glass ball, prevents the radiation from escaping into the surrounding sea. I wondered what happened to the glass ball when they detonated the next 'mega-bomb' just 500 metres from it. It must shatter to pieces, releasing all the radioactivity.

After the test, they drill a second shaft at a cross angle into the cavity to take samples for a more accurate measurement of the explosion yield.

When the French first decided to go underground, they conducted their tests in the outer rim of the atoll, the land portion. Then they moved to the area beneath the lagoon. I supposed this was for a number of reasons: they were running out of room, they did not have to drill so deep, and it was less dangerous; by exploding bombs so close to the outer rim of the volcano they had been creating both lateral and longitudinal faults in the atoll. These faults were viewed by scientists as potential areas for radioactive leakage.

August 26

'No Nukes, No Nukes, No Nukes. We don't want your bomb. Chirac Attack!' This was what we sang to help get us through one of the worst days so far.

A very strong south-east gale blew up with winds steady at 45 knots and gusting to over 60 knots. We took down all sail and put up the storm jib. We tried keeping course, but the seas were very confused and we pounded heavily. Giles said he was expecting the fibreglass yacht to delaminate. The sound of some of the crashes was like being hit by a bus. The whole boat shuddered. We changed course and ran off the wind for a while. This was more comfortable, but it was taking us at great speed to Auckland. That wasn't good enough. We tried again, this time taking the sea head on. We still pounded heavily. We had to slow the boat down to 2–3 knots to allow us to ride each crest and trough smoothly.

To do this we needed to create a drag in the water. We had two tyres on board as an emergency. I had always carried tyres for this purpose, but never needed to use them. Most gales were typically in the direction of sail and it was a matter of running before them under bare poles if necessary.

Giles and I donned our gear and went out in the dark and stormy maelstrom to do it. We sang the Chirac Attack song for encouragement. Seas were breaking over us as we pulled a tyre and line from the aft locker. We sent it astern. The little task, in those conditions, took about 40 minutes. It worked. The boat slowed up, but by the sound of the crashing it wasn't enough.

We decided to put out the second tyre. This time young Paul volunteered to help. He was still seasick and spewed once or twice along the way. I admired his dedication. We pulled in the previous tyre, which took 15 minutes. We then lashed on the second, bigger, tyre and re-deployed them both. VOILA! It worked. We slowed *Joie* up enough to comfortably sail into the strong south-easterly without pounding. We were making 2–4 knots in the general direction we wanted to travel. Inside it was reasonably comfortable. Occasionally a large wave crashed on deck making a loud bang and shuddering the whole boat. This would be followed by a 4–5-second onslaught of a tonne of water as if you were being hosed to death! Swish, swash, gurgle. We were gradually getting accustomed to this alarming sound as our confidence in *Joie* grew.

All areas of the boat were wet. We thought we had watertight hatches. All crew were also wet and there was nowhere to dry out. We slept in wet bunks and in wet clothes. Despite the situation, morale was still reasonably good.

I went on deck to relieve Dennis from his watch. Dennis stayed huddled in the cockpit for a while and talked with me. "Ever try living in a switched on washing machine for five to six days?" Dennis asked. "This is what it's like. We are really getting plastered with these huge seas. It reminds me of tramping: the boat goes up one hill and down the valley, with a brief look around at the top. Every movement is an effort. Do I need this pee? No, hold off! Can I get to the other side of the boat without ramming a wall? And the boat leaks, Lynn. It's all wet and damp."

"All boats leak, Dennis," I said. "It's par for the course. We are sailing in some rough waters at the wrong time of the year. The other boats will be wet too. We just have to put up with it until we get further north into warmer waters."

"You mean to tell me that this is the way it is?" Dennis asked. "I never imagined this. We've filled lots of holes with sealant. The cupboards are full of water, drips are coming down the walls, damp clothes, wet sleeping bags. I mean, if I wasn't wearing poly-prop skivvies, a thick jersey and a two-fibre jacket, I'd get hypothermia and die! I haven't washed since we left. None of us have, and the whole boat reeks of a sickly, sour odour. We can't open the boat up for fear of getting flooded."

Dennis then told me about an earlier near miss with a freak wave. He was still excited about it as he told the story.

"I was sitting here and there were really huge waves coming in, bigger than now, and we were taking them all right, no problem at all, so I wasn't worried. Then we got up on one really big wave, and I suddenly became aware that this was a bit different and big, and I wasn't looking at it, I forget what I was doing, and all of a sudden I look around and this big wave hit us and we went up and up, and oh yeah! I looked ahead and only about 10–15 feet in front of us the water was sheer, it wasn't sloping, it was a vertical face of water about 10 feet high, it looked like a cliff. My eyes stuck out on stalks, and this wall of water just collapsed in front of us! I mean about 15 feet in front. If we had been 10 to 15 feet ahead that thing would have rolled us straight over."

I asked, "Do you really think it would have really rolled us, Dennis?" "Oh it would have," he said. "Trashed us, either pounded right down on top of us or, I would imagine, it would have rolled us. I mean just looking at it, it was like hitting a cliff!"

After I relieved Dennis, he settled down and with renewed ambition went below to make some toasted cheese sandwiches. Because of his unsettled stomach, he had eaten mostly bread since leaving Wellington. In the course of preparing the sandwiches, they ended up all over the galley when a high wave hit the boat. This was the first time I saw Dennis get mad. I thought he had had enough. But he pulled it together and finished the wonderful toasted cheese sandwiches. However, he was too nauseous to eat them and offered them all to us!

It was raining very hard. I was determined to get the Tilley lantern going as a source of heat. The diesel cabin stove would only blow back again in this weather. Again, in part of the haste of leaving, we had stowed the 20-litre container of kerosene in the engine room. I had to don my gear, go outside, descend into the engine room and fetch it. We then had to transfer it into a smaller 4-litre bottle so that it could be used to fill up the Tilley. We executed this manoeuvre in the main cabin with Giles holding the 4-litre container and me pouring the 20-litre one. In the tossing seas, we spilled as expected, but surprisingly very little. The Tilley was fired up and it gave us the simple warmth we needed.

We made no radio contact that evening with any of the Wellington boats. We heard *Chimera*, but they could not hear us. *Chimera* reported 10-metre swells and was on the drogue (a device thrown into the water to create drag and slow the boat down in bad weather).

On the Greenpeace sked, *Sudden Laughter*, the Nelson-based catamaran, reported a problem with her hull lashings and said she was not repairable at sea so they were returning to New Zealand to try and effect repairs. They were also experiencing the same south-east gale that we had. He said his boat was obviously not up to the standard required for the trip. Good night. I went to my wet bunk for some shut-eye.

August 27

We all got a very good sleep last night and Dennis and Giles were raring and ready to go. Young Paul, however, had been mostly bedridden for the last 5 days and unable to participate in ship duties. He did not seem to be coming right, and I insisted he take some seasick pills. He had previously not taken them because they made him dizzy. He finally agreed to take some and soon he was eating food and drinking again.

We continued to beat into 25-knot south-east winds. It was still very uncomfortable, but the crew were in good spirits. I cooked a stew in the pressure cooker. Occasionally we crashed heavily in a sea. We were close-reaching with storm jib and tri-sail and making 5 knots at 80° true. For the thousands of miles we had to go, it was hard sailing. We were looking forward to more favourable winds.

Water was leaking on young Paul's bunk. He was wet, cold and still sick, and we were feeling sorry for him. Dennis and I traced the leak to the stove stack deck plate. We hove-to, to stop *Joie*, then dried out the area with alcohol and caulked it. Paul thanked us for fixing it.

We were unable to contact *New Zealand Maid* or *Kela*, but made contact with *Chimera*. They were a couple of hundred miles behind. They told us that they and *New Zealand Maid* both lost their drogues in the gale. In both situations the shackle connecting the drogue to its line had come undone. "That's strange that both of you would lose them. Must be a design fault," I said. We transmitted our position to *Chimera* and they told us they heard there was a vessel coming all the way from Chile, which would be arriving at Moruroa in a couple of weeks. "That's cool," I said. "I wish I was sailing that direction; all downwind and in a warm latitude!"

Dennis made an attempt at the mess in the engine room. He retrieved the last of the onions, while Giles was good enough to peel and salvage what he could. They were all covered in engine oil and diesel from floating in the bilge. 'Yum, onions from the engine room, with kero-sauce,' I thought. Dennis also saved the oranges, but left the potatoes to keep for another day.

I fired up the Tilley again well before dark just to give us some warmth. We were still wet and cold. Dennis found a small piece of plastic to use on top of the cushions to keep him dry when he slept.

Giles made himself a nice little nest on the starboard bunk behind the lee cloth. He had been reading about the Gambier Islands and persuaded us to sail there as a provisioning, resting and regrouping spot before proceeding on to Moruroa. Not much convincing was required; the other skippers also liked the idea.

The Gambier Islands, also called Mangareva Islands, are situated at the south-eastern extremity of the Tuamotu Archipelago, about 230 nautical miles south-east of Moruroa. They are a group of small coral islands. The group's largest island is the site of the chief settlement, Rikitea. Other islands include Akamaru, Aukena and Taravai. Copra is their principal product. They have a population of about 600 people.

These beautiful Pacific islands have had a horrific history, thanks again to missionaries and the French colonialists. In 1834, a Jesuit missionary, the notorious Father Honoré Laval, settled there and gained control over the king, Maputeoa, to such an extent that he was able to enslave the people and force them to work on large building projects. The ruins of these, including a very big church, are scattered incongruously around the island. His despotic rule was responsible for the deaths of approximately 5000 people and the destruction of the Mangarevan culture.

Then the French Centre for Experiments in the Pacific had a go at them. In 1963, when the French initiated their nuclear testing programme, they dredged massive amounts of coral from the Mangareva lagoon for construction purposes on nearby Moruroa. This activity was blamed for the sudden poisoning of the fish in the lagoon by ciguatera. Humans get ciguatera fish poisoning by eating tropical fish that have fed on a particular algae which grows on damaged or dead coral. The dinoflagellate organism, *Gambierdiscus toxicus*, which causes ciguatera, was actually named after the Gambier Islands, where there was a serious outbreak in 1968. Ciguatera outbreaks are linked to construction work, explosions and dredging, as well as to natural disasters.

It became impossible for the islanders to eat the fish and, with their main source of protein removed, many families began to drift to the main island and to Tahiti. Mangareva is now the only inhabited island of the group. Some of the children living there are said to have extra fingers and toes, deformities which the locals say date from the start of nuclear testing at Moruroa. Patrick Howell, a dentist who later became Minister of Health for French Polynesia, found strontium 90 in the teeth of all the young people in the Gambier Islands.

August 28
Morale was low in the morning as we continued to beat hard into a 30-knot south-east wind. We pounded heavily; the sea was very mixed and confused. We still had storm sails on. Radio contact with *New Zealand Maid*, who were further west, indicated that they had had a wind shift and were able to sail directly east. Our course at best was 70°. Finally, the low pressure area moved south-west and we got the wind shift we wanted. Although many squalls still persisted, we were again moving in the right direction.

By 19.00 the seas dropped and we had a fresh wind from the south. At midnight we put up more sail and began sailing along at 7.5 knots.

Dennis, who had been slightly depressed, had come alive. He was beginning to enjoy the sailing and was a good sailor. I loved talking with him because he had a vivacious philosophical mind.

"Looking back at that gale we just had," he said, "the inner intelligence in my body really went into damage control: It said to me, 'what the f*ck is going on?' The constant motion, sound (whining, moaning, and shrieking wind in the rigging) and the wet and cold made it almost unbearable. My inner intelligence was rather like an observer of it all. If I had the chance, I certainly would have shot home! I thought the other crew would be loving this, but to my surprise they were worse than me! There is kind of a vacuum of time out here where everything seems obscure. You just mix snoozing, eating, relaxing and doing jobs together in the same time warp."

I started the engine to charge the batteries and accidentally bumped the gear shift lever. This engaged the propeller shaft and broke the tie-down cord we used to prevent the propeller shaft from spinning when under sail. I had warned my crew about this, and yet I did it myself! 'Well, I must find a new tie-down cord and re-secure the spinning shaft,' I said to myself.

When I went into the engine room, there seemed to be a fair amount of water. I asked Giles to turn on the bilge pump. He said he did, but the water was still rising rapidly. I thought he might have got the wrong switch, so I asked him again to turn on the pump. He said, "I did. It's on!"

At this point I appreciated that the engine room was flooding and called out: "Emergency! All hands on deck." The water was sloshing over the engine bay and rising quickly. I felt ghastly: we were sinking. 'We're doomed, I thought to myself. This is it.'

For a moment, I did not want to deal with the situation. The engine room was a claustrophobic place. It was small, dark, damp and smelled of oil and diesel. Large volumes of water were sloshing side to side with every ocean swell, making me seasick. I reluctantly crouched down to assess the situation. I was cold, tired, wet and getting wetter as the water rose up over my knees.

Giles put on the hose for the emergency hand pump that we had installed before the trip and began pumping furiously. What a fantastic pump! It pumped 20 gallons per minute and Giles was able to gain slightly on the inflow of water. Soon I was able to find where the leak came from. The bolts that pinned the propeller shaft to the flange had turned loose and the shaft disengaged and slipped back outside the boat. Water was flooding in from the packing gland, which of course had no shaft in it. We had a 2-inch diameter hole in the boat!

I crammed some rags into the hole and Dennis and I capped it with a plastic bag and hose clamp. Without a propeller shaft, we were strictly a sailing vessel. Fortunately, because of the yacht's fin keel and skeg rudder design, the propeller shaft did not fall into the ocean; it was stopped by the skeg. Nevertheless, it was still outside the boat, and we would have to wait for a day of doldrums or until we reach the Gambier Islands to fix it.

We would have to send a diver over the side to push the shaft back inside. I was disappointed we had this problem. I had taken off the flange prior to leaving and had paid marine engineers to re-work the fitting and fasteners. I asked them about pinning the shaft to the flange and they remarked that it was not necessary. Well so much for that advice! We planned to pin it in the Gambier Islands.

I got out the guitar and played some music to cheer up the crew. I felt a new song coming on: the Sailing to Moruroa Blues.

Our position was 38° 48' S, 169° 56' W, and we were cruising along at 7.5 knots.

August 29, 06.45 hours
We found a couple of squid on the deck in the morning. Normally one would find flying fish, not squid of all things! I don't think the ship's phantom cat left them there; the seas were so rough, the squid were deposited on deck when we either 'submarined' through one of the many large seas or when a large wave crashed over the boat. I threw them in the pot and cooked them up. They were small squid, only about 4 inches long. Dennis tried one but he was not impressed when he bit into it and the black ink sac broke and bled down his chin and all over his bowl. I did not care and popped the whole thing into my mouth and chewed it down whole. It was very tasty, ink sac and all. Dennis said "20 000 whales can't be wrong" and continued munching his.

We sailed all day goosewinged, running before a 20-knot westerly. With the wind directly behind us, no water was splashing onto the boat for a change. We got out all the wet cushions and clothes and hung them up everywhere and anywhere we could. The boat looked like a Hong Kong apartment building. As the wind backed north-west we dropped the whisker pole and managed to get the jib wrapped around the forestay. We had to drop the sail to unwind it. After a slight delay, we got under way again, reaching-off at 8 knots.

Young Paul, feeling better, prepared a curry and rice dinner that night. He used three pots and a fry pan to make the meal. It was amusing to watch him juggle the pots and pan to keep their contents from spilling onto the floor in the rolling seas.

We finalised our watch roster: 2 hours on and 6 hours off per crew member.

Nick on *Kela* was keen to go to the Rapa Islands and talked us into going as well. They are a small group of islands, in French territory, about 600 nautical miles south-west of Moruroa. It seemed like an interesting place from a geological and historical point of view, but the entrance is tricky and anchor holding variable according to the cruising guide. We would try to fix our propeller shaft at sea before going in, if we went at all.

The *MV Greenpeace*, Greenpeace's large ocean-going tug, had arrived on scene at Moruroa and they picked up the flotilla roll-call duties from *Rainbow Warrior*. Although they transmitted better than the *Rainbow Warrior*, they did not receive as well. This was a bit disconcerting. They mentioned that they had had long tactical meetings. There were a number of French frigates in the area and, when they flew their helicopter, it was met by three French helicopters. The Greenpeace helicopter was much faster and the pilot, Paula Huckleberry, flew circles around the French helicopters.

August 29, 16.00 hours

	Joie	Kela	NZ Maid	Chimera
Latitude S	38° 32'	36° 54'	36° 58'	36° 53'
Longitude W	163° 55'	166° 13'	165° 37'	165° 54'

We were about 1000 nautical miles out of Wellington and 650 miles north-east of the Chatham Islands. We were about a third of the way to Moruroa.

Winds had been steady from the NW sector and we were making 6.5 knots on a course of 70° true. We planned to run a great circle route to 35° S and 150° W, then proceed directly to Rapa.

Dennis told me that when he was on watch earlier a weak sun poked its head from out of the clouds. He said he happened to put his hand on the deck and, "wonders! It was warm. Simply that." Dennis said, "My reaction was amazing, my heart leapt with a wee stab of joy and I kept putting my hand back to feel it, each time getting the same reaction. It is amazing how we crave such simple comforts, isn't it?"

Giles and I worked on the lyrics of the song Dirty Old Town. We did not remember them all so we made up some of our own words.

August 30

It was a beautiful dawn morning with light winds and easy seas and we were sailing along methodically into the rising sun. Dennis was on watch and I came out to sit with him for a while in the cockpit. The lovely and peaceful morning obviously put him in a bit of a philosophical mood.

He told me a little about some of the Indian philosophy that he had learnt. He said, "It's called the Play of The Gunas, and it is viewed as three forces, qualities or attributes that in equilibrium keep the universe in a balanced state. 'Tamas' represents inertia, inactivity, ignorance, dullness, laziness and so forth; 'Rajas' explains a condition of activity, passion, greed, power, jealousy, rage, high energy, excitement, anger, elation; and 'Sattva' means goodness, purity, knowledge, tranquillity, peace, bliss and happiness which prevails when everything comes together in balance."

"So how does it all work, Dennis?" I asked. Dennis explained, "Well, that bad gale we just had was 'Rajas'. It was a high energy state, and the sea was angry. Now compare the conditions this morning. This is total bliss, a condition of 'Sattva'," he said. "Yeah, I see what you mean," I said. "But what about the third force, 'Tamas'?" He said, "That's what happened to us after that bad-ass gale beat the crap out of us!"

At midnight the wind had virtually died out. We were wallowing a lot but, according to the GPS, still making about 4 knots.

We had our first crew discussion about cooking and doing dishes. From my experience, this always becomes a major bone of contention. There are always those who do not want to make a contribution in this area and it makes those who do a little uptight. My recommendation at the onset of the trip was for those doing the cooking to also do the dishes. Well, two of the crew decided not to cook or wash dishes at all. We finally came to an arrangement that if a person preferred not to cook, then they would volunteer to clean up after. There would no doubt be more discussions on this topic.

MV Greenpeace announced on the radio that a 'European Peace Flotilla', which was organised to arrive on the River Seine with almost 35 million signatures in protest against the tests, had been banned by the French police. The petitions were to be delivered to the quayside at Pont d'Iena, where a human chain of people, including Members of Parliament and other VIPs from around the world, would carry them to the Elysee Palace, taking the message to President Chirac. The French Government, however, outlawed it because they claimed a human chain would cause a public disturbance! The protesters tried to carry on anyway, but the police intervened. They stopped the protest flotilla from coming up the Seine and broke the human chain. In the process some 100 people were arrested.

MV Greenpeace also broadcast something to the effect that French officials had accused Greenpeace of using excessive power to influence the protest flotilla.

Young Paul inspected the vacuum-packed meat in the bilge only to find that two bags containing over 6 kilograms of top sirloin steak had broken and were awash with bilge water. Vacuum-packed meat could last up to a month without refrigeration providing, of course, the seal was not broken. Not expecting to find any butcher shops at Moruroa, I volunteered to wash the meat down, and salt and dry it to make beef jerky. There was very strong 'Rajas' from both Pauls about this. They insisted that it be thrown away, as if it was a strong religious belief of theirs. Dennis was amazed at this, and asked them to relax a bit. "You don't have to eat any of it if you don't want to," he said. "So why are you both so upset?" Despite Dennis's arbitration in the matter, the 'Rajas' continued. I decided to continue with the salvage and cut into the meat. It was fine and I even ate some raw to test it. I sliced it up, salted it in a bucket and prepared to dry it in the sun and wind the next day.

Dennis cooked up a meal of vegies and steak while I began preparations for reconnecting the propeller shaft. I disconnected the propeller shaft flange from the transmission. I then removed and tapered the ends of the shaft-seat bolts so that they would actually fit tightly into the shaft once we push it back in place. We would also need to drill out the shaft hole-seats a little more so that our newly manufactured bolts would fit snugly.

Giles spent an hour hand drilling a small hole through the heads of both bolts so that we could secure them with a wire and thus prevent them from turning loose again. The hand drill, which Dennis purchased for $80 (under protest) before leaving, had already paid for itself.

August 31

We caught our first tuna! I filleted it, Dennis fried some up and young Paul made sushi. We had been running before a south-west wind of 20 knots. Aries had some difficulty holding course and would need to be looked into. Perhaps a fishing line or other debris was caught in the paddle.

We were about half way to Moruroa as the crow flies; it was our tenth day at sea. I expected our speed to slow as we moved north into variable winds. We planned for a 21-day sail to the test site, but it could take us longer.

Nikao Radio in Rarotonga had taken over the flotilla roll-call as a joint arrangement between the marine station at Rarotonga and the New Zealand Amateur Radio Association. The Association set up a network across New Zealand with one member, 'Rib', transmitting from the Nikao base to send free messages to and from the flotilla fleet and their families back home. It was a tremendous effort and highly appreciated by the flotilla. They also provided excellent weather forecasts and sea condition reports.

There were currently prevailing north-east winds at the Rapa Islands. This meant that if we stopped at Rapa, we would need to beat directly into the wind when we carried on to Moruroa. I discussed this situation with the other skippers.

September 1

Strong south-westerlies continued. We were running before them goosewinged. Dennis, who was on night watch, yelled alarmingly, "Something's wrong with the steering! I'm barely able to control the course. I need some help up here!" It was pitch black outside and almost impossible to hand steer in the large swells.

The problem was caused by the Aries deck pulley assembly coming loose from the deck. I jury-rigged a temporary repair while Dennis continued to hand steer. It took about 45 minutes to make the repair, and afterwards Dennis remarked how invaluable the self-steering was: "It would be sheer pain and misery and even dangerous if we had to hand steer while on night watch in these conditions." In the morning I completed a proper repair, which involved drilling larger holes and through-bolting the assembly to the deck.

Dennis sorted out the food drawers and strictly devoted one to 'munchies'. He filtered through all our stores, and organised things such as instant soups, muesli bars, sweets, cookies, hot chocolate, tea and coffee so they were easily accessible to the night watch crew.

New Zealand Maid and *Kela* were about 90 nautical miles behind us. Our relative latitudes were closing as we proceeded north slightly and they came slightly south. Because of the prevailing NE winds at French Polynesia, we would give Rapa a miss and keep going east while we could. Nick, Jon and Gary agreed.

We heard that the 16-tonne *Te-Au-O-Tonga*, a traditional 22-metre twin-hulled sailing canoe, and her 18 Polynesian crew had finally arrived at Moruroa from the Cook Islands after a 13-day voyage. They had had to turn back on their first attempt because of bad weather, and were towed a good part of the way by their escort, a Cook Islands patrol boat.

At the exclusion zone, the crew performed a 'haka', or menacing war dance, stamping their feet viciously on the canoe's wooden deck. A haka, delivered with conviction by a group of men, is a very powerful and frightening spectacle. *Te-Au-O-Tonga* was not equipped for a long stay and after beating 1100 nautical miles against the SE Trades and spending only 7 hours on site they headed back to Rarotonga. The canoe's skipper said they were most grateful that all of the protest ships were going there to fight for their home environment. He accused France of polluting the South Pacific and recalled ancient times when Polynesian sailing craft like *Te-Au-O-Tonga* had the pristine ocean all to themselves.

We heard from Nick, who managed to do a live broadcast on More FM radio and Capital TV's telethon from his powerful radio transmitter. He said that More FM had raised $10,000 for us. Wow! That took a bit of pressure off us financially.

September 2

We sailed 185 nautical miles in the last 24 hours. Dennis was in another one of his romantic philosophical moods. He really missed Marianne, his partner, and he often contemplated his relationship with her in his new ocean environment. "East, east, always east!" he said to me. "It's really amazing how you can travel day after day in one direction and nothing seems different; just sea and more sea, no ships. Only the birds change. I'm surprised we still have them with us. We're over half way to Moruroa now. Look at those big albatrosses and the smaller birds that look too small to survive out here.

"I watched two small ones the other day when it was bleak and stormy and the sheer loneliness and 'wasteness' of the ocean seemed immense. Yet there they were; these two creatures apparently quite at home and I wondered if they had anything in common with me, and then it struck me that they had companionship. Was that why there were two? I could relate to that. It gave me a sort of an affection for them, a little bond."

I was waiting for Dennis to change the subject from his romantic birds to an explanation of the stars, for they did not seem right for us that day. We had a series of events that kept us very busy. To begin, I tried to start the engine to charge the batteries and got an 'ug-ug' sound and no start! Something had obviously gone wrong with the batteries and the expensive electrical rewiring I had done before leaving.

I popped into the engine room and tested the batteries with my hydrometer. The service batteries, which get the main charge first under the new system, were completely flat. Both batteries (75 amp–hours) were brand new before leaving. When I tested my starting battery it was 3/4 full charge. This one was separated from the service batteries and dedicated for engine starting. Even so, the engine would not turn over.

So out came the starter motor. Dennis and I pulled it to bits, re-greased it and sanded down the brushes. It had got very wet when the engine room last flooded. I then disconnected the new three-step regulator, which I deduced was the cause of the battery drain, and re-mounted the old regulator. VA-ROOM! The engine fired over and we were able to charge the batteries again. The charge rate, however, was very unsteady. I suspected a compatibility problem between the old voltage regulator and the new alternator, but at least we were able to get some juice back into the batteries.

When such things happen in the open sea, far away from land, one gets a very strong feeling of anxiety, of 'lostness', of defeat. Mishaps in harbour were no problem; you could take all the time you needed and find experts to consult. But when your engine goes 'ug' in the middle of the Pacific, your stomach does the same. Your mind begins to think the worst: 'How will we be able to transmit on the radio? Everyone will think we are lost at sea.' Lethargy sets in in a big way and you just want to ignore the problem and go to your bunk. 'But there's no one else out here to fix it, dummy; it's your responsibility', someone in your head tells you. Eventually that someone pulls you up by your boot straps and you deal with the situation.

Our next episode that day occurred when we needed to pole out the sail and run before the 20-knot south-westerly. Giles noticed that the whisker pole was badly bent and broken. It was probably bent in the last gale, when we took tonnes of water on the deck. Fortunately, and at the last moment before leaving, I sought out and purchased two very large U-bolts. At the time, I thought we could use them for attaching a sheet of plywood to the whisker pole for use as an emergency rudder.

After straightening out the pole, I found a piece of aluminium angle and braced it across the weakened section of the pole. We clamped it hard in place with the two U-bolts. It secured the break well and was very strong. Yes! We could again pole out the front sail and run before the wind on the desired course of 80° true.

Young Paul got a message from Nikao Radio (Rarotonga), which was relayed by *Kela*. The message was from his partner Catherine who said, 'Missing you, the baby is kicking strongly. It is hard without you. See you in Papeete end of September.' We teased Paul as to what she really meant by saying 'it is hard without you'. Paul ignored our jokes. He was expecting his first son to be born and was very content to receive the message. He remarked, "I am in the middle of the Pacific and can still get a message from Catherine." He was very satisfied and went back to sleep.

I thought back to a point earlier in the day when, in the middle of servicing the starter motor, Dennis said, "We should let the bloody French have their bomb. It would be a damn sight easier." The stress of the day and all the mishaps and repairs had obviously taken their toll. However, the day ended on a good note with young Paul cooking up a wonderful pumpkin and vegie soup for dinner in the pressure cooker. It was delicious and hit the spot!

September 3

We had our second boat meeting. The agenda was: watches, boat chores, food consumption, water conservation and collection.

There is a phenomenon that attacks people at sea. I call it 'boat lethargy', and it has surfaced on every long passage I have taken. Crew members tend to lose their motivation and enthusiasm and are happy just to stay in their bunks all day. They get lazy and do nothing. I believe boat lethargy is caused partly by the physical motion of the vessel, which has the combined effect of rocking one to sleep and making even the smallest task difficult.

During the meeting we talked about the importance of keeping good watches and not dozing off. It was difficult convincing the crew of the seriousness of this, as we had not seen one vessel in the 12 days since we left. We talked about everyone overcoming the boat lethargy and contributing to the chores. Our fresh produce was rotting, because we were not eating it first. Finally, we discovered that we had only one third of a tank of water left; about 140 litres. We needed to conserve water and try to collect rain water at the first opportunity.

We heard the French were about to explode their first test any day now. We would probably miss it. We also heard that a group of six New Zealand Members of Parliament, including NZ First leader Winston Peters, National's John Carter and Labour's Pauline Gardiner, would go to Papeete to take part in an anti-nuclear protest. Politicians from all around the world would be joining the protest.

Triptych had arrived on site at Moruroa. They had suffered damage to their mast, propeller, engine and halyard, and were low on fuel and water. They received assistance from *Tui*. This was a relief to hear, and it appeared that the Government had relaxed *Tui*'s original instructions of a hands-off approach to the flotilla.

Strong north sector winds continued at 25 knots with gusts to over 30. We sailed 160 nautical miles in 24 hours: just under 7 knots average speed. We maintained a course of 80° true and climbed to 36° S latitude, or just under the latitude of Whangarei, New Zealand.

Sailing was rough with rain squalls and high winds. *Joie* occasionally took a big hit by a wave.

September 4

	Joie	*Kela & NZ Maid*	*Chimera*
Latitude S	35° 43'	35° 30'	35° 53'
Longitude W	146° 29'	148° 11'	148° 13'

Kela, *New Zealand Maid* and *Chimera* constantly adjusted their speeds and courses to keep reasonably together. We heard they had been swapping food on some of the better days. *Kela* even managed to transfer five 20-litre containers of water to *New Zealand Maid* on one pleasant day.

We heard from Greenpeace that two women and two men went into Moruroa in an inflatable. They were apprehended in the lagoon by the French military and flown to Papeete.

Later in the day we heard reports that both *MV Greenpeace* and *Rainbow Warrior* were seized by the French military.

I made a fruit salad for breakfast and a corned beef stew for lunch. Dennis cooked a vegie and scalloped potato dish for dinner. Dennis and I were the chief cooks and we both laughed at our preoccupation with what to prepare for the next meal. All we thought about was eating and the skeds; they were the highlights of the day.

The potatoes were going rotten so Dennis hung them out in the breeze to dry. It was difficult to find a dry spot on the boat as we were heading into 28–30 knot north-westerlies. The two Pauls cleaned out the head, vegie basket and swept the floor. Young Paul had been sick again and in bed most of the day.

We were unable to receive any AM/FM radio broadcasts in the middle of the Pacific, but heard a few bits on the SSB radio. Giles heard fishermen talking about the yachts that had already arrived at Moruroa. Some had gone into the zone, were arrested and escorted back outside the 12-mile limit. It also appeared that Greenpeace had made another move with four people in a rubber raft. They were arrested and sent to Papeete.

Both *Chimera* and *Kela* reported their freezers had stopped working. Gary said on the radio, "Well, I guess they had to do without them in the old days." I wanted to respond saying that neither *Joie* nor *New Zealand Maid* had freezers, but hesitated from doing so. Dennis joked that *Chimera* should use their freezer as a sea anchor since they had lost their drogue in the last gale.

Jon on *New Zealand Maid* reported that he had a friend in Golden Bay with a shore station transmitting license with whom he was in contact via the radio. His friend would be happy to pass on any messages we had for our families. *Joie's* radio was unable to transmit that far, so we all drafted our messages to give to Jon, who would relay them on. Young Paul was so excited that he wrote a two page letter to Catherine. The rest of us laughed and suggested that he cut it down to no more than one short paragraph. It was very difficult to relay long messages via SSB radio. Reception was often marginal, and every few words were repeated sometimes three or four times to make sure they were heard properly. In the end our messages went something like this:

'All is well, all is well. We are over half way there. Missing you, missing you. Will call from Papeete on arrival. Love from the *Joie*.'

September 5

	Joie	*Kela*	*NZ Maid*	*Chimera*
Latitude S	34° 08'	33° 54'	33° 58'	34° 27'
Longitude W	143° 46'	146° 28'	145° 53'	145° 18'

Nick confirmed that two Zodiacs had gone into the lagoon and that both Greenpeace ships had been seized, with steering cables and communications cut. They were being towed to one of the French archipelago islands.

New Zealand Maid confirmed our messages had got through 'with great excitement' from our families.

Kela reported taking a large wave, which slammed them on their side. They also did some damage to their mainsail. We also took a large 'greenie', which slammed into and on the top of us, causing water to squirt through every conceivable crevice. The two Pauls reduced sail in the middle of the night.

On the sked we heard that the French had exploded their first bomb of the series. It was about the size of the one dropped on Hiroshima. All French Polynesia was in an uproar and there was rioting. The international community was also in an uproar.

The Greenpeace vessel *Manutea* arrived at Moruroa and her crew transmitted an update of the situation. They confirmed that the French had gone ahead with an estimated 20-kilotonne explosion at Moruroa, but that it had been delayed by two Greenpeace activists who had hidden on the island. They reported that international pressure on the French Government was increasing dramatically.

Also, 200 people working at Moruroa went on strike.

We all felt a bit empty inside, as though the party had gone on without us. We were very disappointed and felt useless. If we had been on site, at least we could have put on our black shirts and gone to the edge of the zone to mourn or something. But there we were, still some 1000 miles away from the atoll.

There was one consolation, however; the weather had improved. The sun was a blessing. We opened up the whole boat: all hatches and portlights, and put all the wet clothes and cushions on the deck to dry further. At one stage *Joie* looked like a produce shop. Dennis cleaned all the spuds and oranges that had been in the bilge and laid them all on the deck to dry. I also had the home-made beef jerky out drying in the sun.

CHAPTER 6

To Moruroa: the French in Polynesia

If the British had got their act together 230 years ago, the territory of Polynesia would probably have passed through its colonial phase and become independent like Fiji, Kiribati and Tonga. Captain Samuel Wallis actually took possession of Tahiti in the name of George III in 1767. English missionaries arrived 30 years later. In the 1830s Queen Pomare and leading chiefs asked Queen Victoria to place Tahiti under British protection.

By then, though, the British had their hands full in New Zealand, Australia and elsewhere. Furthermore, who would want to acquire a collection of tiny palm islands and coral reefs with no riches to offer, while there were other lands in Africa and Asia with an abundance of gold, precious stones, ebony, spices and other natural resources?

The French Government learned something from Britain when it had taken possession of Australia solely for the purpose of using it as a dumping ground for its surplus convicts. French Admiral Dupetit-Thouars, who had spent a few days in the Marquesas Islands in 1838, warmly recommended them as ideally suited for that purpose. The Marquesas are an island group some 1000 nautical miles north of Tahiti, and consist of 10 fertile volcanic islands. Not only did they reside thousands of miles from the nearest continents, they were also said to be inhabited by savage cannibals, a disincentive to escape from the safety of the prison!

Liking the idea, the French Government sent Admiral Dupetit-Thouars to take possession of the Marquesas. He then sailed to Tahiti and annexed that island as well, though he had no orders to do so. The London Missionary Society, well established in Tahiti, cried foul play, but soon realised that the French were there to stay. Surrounding islands were eventually annexed and the area became a French protectorate.

Perhaps the French colonial administrators had not changed much in the 150 years that they had controlled these islands. I personally had received a strong taste of the 'French way' of doing things when I sailed through Polynesia in 1981 on my trip from Alaska to New Zealand. It was a memorable experience that tainted my opinion of these administrators. I could still vividly recall the incident.

We had arrived in the Marquesas after an 18-day non-stop sail from Cabo San Lucas, Mexico. After clearing customs, my crew and I sailed to a small island called Tahu Ata. It was a beautiful post-card picture island with a lovely anchorage. The beach consisted of white sand and was lined with coconut palms. From the beach, the island grew to a height of around 1000 feet with flowing green hills and mountains.

There were two French cruising yachts already anchored in the bay. I swam over to one of the boats and met Alain and Marie. They told me all about the wonderful paradise. There were lots of coconuts, breadfruit and oranges to eat and there were even wild goats in the hills. They said goats were introduced by the early European explorers – Cook, Bougainville, and Bligh – and since have grown to large numbers.

Because many of the local fish were affected by ciguatera and were poisonous to eat and since we had not had fresh meat since leaving Mexico, we decided to go for a goat hunt. We saw a herd of wild goats on the hill above us and made a plan. Forrest and Chris (my crew) were to hike around the back of the hill and I would go up the front with the gun. They would scare the goats my way and I would blast one. It was very difficult climbing through the dense jungle-like bush and clinging vines, and it was very hot and humid. Our plan was successful and I bagged a small goat.

That evening we had eleven people for a wonderful spit-roast barbecue on the beach. Two beautiful French girls knew how to best cook the goat. They tenderised it by poking it with a knife and massaged it with butter and garlic salt. A bottle of rum and wine were consumed during the bacchanalian delight. We ate goat all evening and it tasted better as the night went on. Needless to say, there were many good sailing stories told that night around the campfire. 'This is what life was all about. This is heaven,' I thought to myself.

The next morning, the French gendarme arrived in a small powerboat and inspected our barbecue pit. I saw him pick out some bones and put them in a sack. He then told us that all four yachts had to go back to Nukuhiva, the main administrative island. "Oh hell, we're in trouble now," I said to Forrest and Chris. "Maybe wild goat hunting isn't allowed here."

On arrival, the gendarme told us that he had received a telegram from the Mayor of Tahu Ata Island saying that his prize pig was missing, and that he had accused us of shooting and eating it. Pigs are a symbol of wealth and status in the islands, and this was therefore a very serious accusation. We did not even realise anyone lived on the island, but were relieved to hear it was a matter of a missing pig. We were in the clear.

We were told that all boats were under investigation and our boat papers and passports were confiscated. We were not allowed to leave the harbour. In other words, we were under boat arrest. Then the interrogations began.

It appeared that the French gendarme had made an overriding decision that we were guilty and developed a ploy to cement in the verdict. First of all, someone leaked the story to the main newspaper in Papeete (*Le Nouvelles*) and we were prosecuted and tried on the front page news: 'YACHTIES PILLAGE MARQUESAS ISLANDS AND KILL MAYOR'S PIG.'

At this point we were getting a little worried. Chris still remembered some of his high school French and together we prepared a signed statement. We explained that we were hungry for some fresh meat and took only one wild goat to feed many people. We pleaded ignorance, were remorseful, and apologised. We offered to pay for the goat. But we insisted that we did not kill the Mayor's pig.

We then saw the second part of the ploy. I was asked to go to the gendarme's office to make a declaration. After interrogating me at length in English, the gendarme typed up a declaration in French for me to sign. He knew that I did not speak French. Before signing it, I asked if he could translate it back to me. He did so, and it was pretty much what I had said, so I signed it.

They then asked Alain, the skipper of the French yacht, to come in to make a declaration. They tried to get Alain to admit that I had shot the pig. When he denied it, they showed him my signed declaration. Alain was so surprised and concerned that after his interrogation he ran back and told me that I had been tricked. The gendarme deceived me into signing a false declaration saying that I had shot the Mayor's pig. The slimy, scummy little bastard!

The French gendarme had all the 'evidence' he needed to do me in: an accusation which we never saw, from the island's Mayor, who no doubt was a highly regarded man; bones taken from our barbecue pit; a strong publicity campaign in the local news; and my signed confession. I was very worried and totally dazzled by how this had all been manipulated by the French gendarme. He never even advised me of my rights for legal representation. This was my next priority, but there were no lawyers there!

The next day, the gendarme's assistant came out to the boat. His name was Peter. He was a big and strong Polynesian man, a wonderful person with a heart of gold. He befriended us during this whole ordeal and believed in our innocence all along. He said he had some news for us. He was trying to keep a very stern face, and said, "We have received another telegram from the Mayor of Tahu Ata." 'Oh no,' I thought, 'this would be more bad news.' Peter then broke out in a wide grin and said, "the Mayor's pig came back home!" He then slapped me on the back hard enough to knock me forward. "Case closed," he said beaming from ear to ear. He was very happy for us. I was ecstatic; I couldn't believe it. "So the pig miraculously returned from the ashes of the scapegoat, did it?" I asked. We were free to go.

The gendarme neither apologised for his accusations and underhanded behaviour, nor did he tell us of any telegram conveying apologies from the Mayor of Tahu Ata. When we finally arrive in Papeete, I met with a journalist of the *Le Nouvelles* paper and they printed a very large retraction article.

Throughout our stay in French Polynesia in 1981, we sensed a strong animosity between the Polynesians and the French administrators. We were told by the locals that the French had very strong control and repressed them. On a number of occasions, we were approached by people asking if we had any guns or ammunition for sale. It appeared that some of the younger men in particular were building up arms in preparation for a possible revolution. Our presence was often initially rejected by the local Polynesians until they learned that we were not Frenchmen. Then they would welcome us into their homes to explain their plight under French colonial rule. They craved the opportunity to speak and learn from us.

Now, here I was again, some 14 years later, on my way back to French Polynesia. The decision by Jacques Chirac to resume nuclear testing was proof that France's colonial hold on the area was as strong as ever. He made that decision without asking the people of French Polynesia.

Obviously, the animosity between the French and Polynesians had not diminished. However, this time I felt I could make a contribution toward helping these wonderful islanders with their situation.

As we sped our way along the high seas, we dampened our anxiety by listening to the Greenpeace radio skeds and reading much of the material we had brought with us. Included among this was an information pack that the Auckland flotilla office had assembled for all the yachts going. It was not to be opened until out at sea.

Inside was a collection of information about the history of the islands we were going to, as well as flotilla tactical and communications plans. There were also 'secret' maps of the islands of Moruroa and Fangataufa with overlays of the cities of Auckland and Wellington on them. 'Great idea,' I thought to myself. This way we could radio to each other and say things like, 'we're at the Botanical Gardens, and moving towards Vivian Street', and the French military would not be able to understand what we were talking about.

The packet contained other information about the history of Moruroa and French nuclear colonialism of Polynesia, which cemented the importance of what we were doing.

Since World War II, colonialism had become the subject of intense moral and political controversy. Many former colonies had depicted colonialism as a system of exploitation, imposed on them by stronger powers, which resulted in economic slums, racial conflict and cultural disorder. In a matter of three decades since World War II, the colonial empires, built over a number of centuries, were almost totally dismantled. It is interesting to note that all the colonies of other major powers – the US, Britain, Spain, Portugal and Belgium – won their independence, but the French Government insisted on holding on to their Pacific Islands colonies. What were their motives?

In the early 1960s, The Territorial Assembly (Polynesian Parliament in Tahiti) did not welcome the tests, and leaders of a pro-independence party that had a majority at the time wrote to scientists all around the world for advice about the health risks of nuclear testing. The French Government, however, maintained political control over the Territorial Assembly and subjected those campaigning for independence or opposing the nuclear programme to imprisonment, surveillance and harassment, as well as economic and political pressure. This seemed to be the way the French colonial administrators operated.

French officials maintained that the tests were completely safe and that that they would result in no radiation leakage and no ecological damage or threat to human health. Japanese Prime Minister Tomiichi Murayama asked French President Jacques Chirac why, if the tests were so safe, he did not conduct them in France.

One would have to question the French Government's sincerity in monitoring and protecting the health of the indigenous people and others involved in its nuclear experiments programme during the long testing period. Although scientific teams had in the past been allowed to make limited tests on the island of Moruroa, there had been no truly independent assessment.

Furthermore, no scientific mission had ever been allowed on Fangataufa, which was believed to still be contaminated from earlier atmospheric tests where nuclear devices were detonated at sea level. Also, no independent health assessment of the people of French Polynesia had been allowed.

In May 1963, the French Governor of Polynesia wrote to the Speaker of the Territorial Assembly and said, 'I should like to repeat my assurances here, in the name of the Republic, that all necessary measures are being taken to guarantee that the population will not suffer in the slightest degree from the scheduled experiments.' Yet later that year, the French administration suddenly stopped publishing French Polynesian public health statistics.

This was a country subjected to some 187 nuclear explosions over the previous 30 years. A team of three doctors representing the international movement of Médecins Sans Frontières studied the situation in 1995 and these were some of their findings:

• The French administration began a register of cancer cases in 1985, nearly 20 years after the testing began;
• There was no register of congenital malformations;
• For two of the island groups in close proximity to Moruroa (Tureia and Gambier), no data on the levels of radioactivity during the period of atmospheric tests was available to the public. Furthermore, there was never any active medical follow-up of these islanders, with a view to early detection of cancer or otherwise;
• There was no information on health outcomes of the 13 000 people who worked on Moruroa or Fangataufa, nor was there any long-term medical follow-up of Polynesian bomb workers and their families.
• There was no publicly available information regarding radiation levels released into the air and water by the tests.

There simply was no reliable information available about the impact of these tests on either the people or the environment.

Jacques Cousteau, who was allowed to study Moruroa atoll for 3 days in 1987, found solid evidence of structural damage, including spectacular fractures, cracks and fissures, dead coral and subsidence of up to 2 metres in parts of the atoll's surface. He also discovered traces of the short-lived radioactive poison iodine 131 in samples of plankton taken at the atoll, indicating venting of bomb waste into the lagoon. This caused him to report that, since the test site was entirely surrounded by water, an atoll was the 'worst choice' for containment of radioactive waste.

With the announcement of the resumption of testing at Moruroa, Cousteau resigned his position from a Presidential environmental commission. In a letter to Chirac he wrote, 'The future of our descendants will only be acceptable in a climate of tolerance... The development of new atomic weapons systems such as submarine launchers, or testing (underground or in the laboratory), serves to encourage non-nuclear states to no longer adhere to the non–proliferation treaty.' He urged Chirac 'to do everything to enable France to contribute actively to outlawing atomic weapons'.

When the French were forced to switch to underground testing, there was only a 25-kilometre stretch of land on the outer rim of the atoll available at Moruroa. Therefore, the test beds had to be positioned very close together, separated by only 500 to 1000 metres. But because the shafts were all drilled along the edge of the atoll, they were always too close to the outer wall of the volcano at their point of detonation.

Incredibly, the French CEP lacked the necessary diving equipment to observe the nature and extent of the damage done to the foundation of the atoll, and to examine the amount of leakage and seepage that occurred each time a bomb was detonated. They would be able to honestly say that no leakage or seepage had been observed.

There was no denying that the atoll had been cracked by the underground testing. Some cracks found in the coral crown were several kilometres long and more than 3 metres wide. Some of the larger fissures, which were the most significant evidence of the damage to the atoll, had been covered up by filling them in with cement.

Some scientists worried that, with so many explosions in a confined space, the cracks that surrounded the blast cavities would eventually propagate far enough to connect with one another. Such a scenario could open the system, allowing radioactive material to pour into the ocean and the atmosphere. Some had suggested that the island could just split up. It was like a block of Swiss cheese!

French officials claimed that the cracks were only in the upper levels of coral, not in the lower levels of basalt where the nuclear devices were exploded. However, no details were given of how any checks were made, either for cracks in the basalt or for radioactive leakage.

At times, news of accidents at Moruroa came to the surface. In 1976, a short notice was published in *Le Journal de Tahiti*:

'According to persistent rumours, the last underground test, undertaken about a month ago, has been far from successful. In fact, the radioactive gas produced by the explosion did not escape along the predicted path, and the technicians are still trying to figure out what happened to it. The French CEP officials refuse, as usual, to give any information, nor do they want to make a comment.'

Where could it have gone, but into the ocean! At least three times, detonations near the rim of the atoll resulted in chunks of the volcano falling off into the ocean, with a probable release of radiation. In one incident, a nuclear device got stuck when it was being lowered into the shaft. It jammed at a depth of 390 metres, near the outer rim of the atoll. It was supposed to be lowered to a depth of 800 metres.

It could not be moved, so the French, deciding not to waste the $1.6 million or so it cost to conduct each test, detonated it where it was stuck. The explosion blew an estimated one million cubic metres of coral and rock from the side of the volcano, creating a tidal wave that washed over a portion of the atoll then spread throughout the Tuamotus. The wave overturned several vehicles, injuring the men inside.

The authorities had also admitted the presence of a sizeable quantity of plutonium in the sediment of Moruroa, the result of an accident when a bomb broke open without exploding.

In 1981, another major disaster occurred. It was caused by a large cyclone that ravaged the area. It had been customary over a number of years to store all sorts of radioactive waste – metal scrap, wood, plastic bags, clothes and so on – in a huge dump on the north coast of the island. When the cyclone hit, heavy seas broke over the atoll and swept the irradiated rubbish into the lagoon, seriously contaminating it.

September 7

Becalmed all night. In the morning we decided to fix the propeller shaft, as these were the weather conditions we had been waiting for. The other boats had been under motor and were about the same distance from Moruroa as we were, although further west of us. I got young Paul out of his bunk to do the dive.

Psychologically, it can be a strange feeling jumping into the water in the middle of the ocean. The bottom was a few miles down and one never knew what strange creatures lurked about the boat, especially since it had been becalmed. Of course we took the opportunity to 'pump prime' young Paul with jokes about the great white shark waiting for him. What added to the atmosphere was that half an hour earlier something very big hit our fishing line and stripped it as though we'd hooked up on a 10-ton log!

Young Paul had been thinking of the dive since the day the propeller shaft fell out. He was very nervous but he overcame his fears, donned his diving gear and bravely plunged over the side.

Dennis and I removed the stowage from the engine room and lifted the fuel tank so that we could work on the job properly. We pulled the rag stuffing from the hole and sea water gushed in at great force. We put a plastic lid on the hole and held it tight while giving instructions to young Paul, who was in the water, to push the shaft back in. He complained that his regulator was leaking. He came back on deck, took off his tank and said he would do the job by free diving.

It seemed like forever as Dennis and I took turns holding the ocean out! Paul finally got back into the water and pushed the shaft in. With the shaft in place we hand-drilled the shaft bolt seat holes to make them deeper. We then had to push the shaft out again so that we could re-mount the shaft flange onto the transmission. With the flange in place, young Paul jumped into the ocean again to push the shaft back in for the final time.

Dennis and I fastened the shaft to the flange, making sure to wire in the nuts so they could not unwind again. We put the fuel tank back in place and re-stowed the engine room. We were a motor vessel again! We motored on for 2 hours, under a light south-east wind to test things out. All was well.

We finally made contact with *Kela*, which was 30 miles ahead of us and slightly to the east. They had motored all night as we wallowed in the sea. They agreed to relay a press release that Dennis and I composed to *New Zealand Maid*. The *New Zealand Maid* would then relay it to their contact in Golden Bay, who would telephone it through to Wellington. It was amazingly complicated to communicate from the middle of the Pacific. Before we left, a landlubber had asked me if I would be taking my cell-phone so we could stay in touch. "Right," I laughed!

The press release read as follows:

'After sailing 2200 nautical miles, the Wellington Peace Flotilla are 600 miles from Moruroa. The Flotilla is disappointed with the French action to continue with the testing, and this has strengthened our resolve to continue on to Moruroa to protest against further tests.'

We were 514 nautical miles from Moruroa and the crew was becoming more anxious. There was a high sense of elation as we headed directly north to our last navigational way point. There were lots of smiles and we jumped up and down like anxious children. Giles celebrated with a few cans of brew and ended up singing us to death all night! I had to join him. I got out the guitar and harmonica and we sang a few tunes together.

We had two tuna on our lines but lost them both on retrieving them. We were ready for another tuna feed. All our meat was gone, much of it spoiled. The bread was all gone. It was getting a lot warmer and our heavy-weather clothing was coming off.

Now that we were getting close to Moruroa, I got out some of the material we brought with us to read about our upcoming home. One of the things that worried me a bit was the risk of radiation from staying there too long. Would I die of leukaemia 2 years after this expedition? William Wilson from the school of medicine at the University of Auckland produced a special paper for us called *Peace Flotilla: Radiation Hazards*. I read it with interest and his conclusions about the risks for the Peace Flotilla were very reassuring:

On all three of the above counts, the radiation dose you can expect to receive on your voyage to Moruroa will be less than if you had stayed in NZ. There would certainly be no risk of additional radiation exposure if you stay outside the 12-mile limit.

The level of radiation contamination on most areas of the atoll itself, and in the lagoon, appears to be very low but has not been studied adequately. Should you enter the lagoon or set foot on the atoll, there is some risk of exposure to additional radiation. While it is not possible to assess this risk in a quantitative manner, clearly the exposure would be exceedingly small for a visit of short duration: people do live and work on the atoll for long periods of time.

When nuclear weapons are tested there is always the possibility of a catastrophic accident, but the chance of this occurring is extremely low. An accident on a scale large enough to result in significant exposure to boats outside the 12-mile limit is very difficult to imagine, but should such an event occur I would expect that the information would be available to the flotilla very quickly. The appropriate response would be to sail out of the area immediately, bearing in mind that the major source of contamination would be down wind of the atoll. If any boats did become exposed to fallout, the exposure could be lessened by battening down the hatches, donning wet-weather gear (for later disposal) and sluicing down the superstructure with buckets of sea-water. However, the possibility of such an event is so exceedingly remote that it makes little sense to develop elaborate plans for such a contingency.

In conclusion, any risks resulting from radiation exposure during the expedition would be trivial in comparison with the normal risks of putting to sea in small boats!

I wondered whether Greenpeace hired Mr Wilson to write all these nice things about the radiation risks at Moruroa to make sure we would all show up. It sounds like a lovely place for a picnic!

September 8

The other three boats were sailing in sight of each other, ready to help *Chimera*, which had only one bolt left holding her rudder flange together. It would have been a serious matter if the rudder fell off. The three boats angled north-east earlier than we had at the last south-west gale and we were all trying to converge before reaching Moruroa. Nick and Jon offered the loan of a rechargeable drill to help with our propeller shaft problem. We were happy to report that we had already fixed it with our hand drill and young Paul's brave diving efforts.

Nick said that he had heard that Papeete airport terminal had been burnt. Some aircraft, including Air New Zealand craft, were damaged. The streets were in riot, and another 200 military personnel were arriving at Papeete. "Unbelievable," I said. I never thought this would ever happen. This was an important development that gave us the assurance that the local people were behind us in the protest.

We were told by *New Zealand Maid* that two letters would be delivered to us by the French Commander at Moruroa upon arrival. One letter would acknowledge our right to a peaceful protest and the other would refuse us permission to make innocent passage between Moruroa and Fangataufa atolls. I was not sure what the latter one was all about, but Dennis and I agreed that we would draft our own letter to the Commander in exchange.

Messages came in via *Kela* from Nikao Radio: Catherine said her cat was lost and she was having a hard time with the pig; Wellington Flotilla Office asked for information on our location and wanted press release material; Dennis's daughter, Mandy, had a good 21st birthday and asked for a $5,000 loan from Dennis!

The Greenpeace vessel *Manutea* gave a campaign update. They reported that 19 people, including eight members of parliament, seven journalists, two Austrian environmentalists and two Greenpeace crew, from ten different countries (the UK, Italy, Spain, Germany, the US, Austria, Japan, Sweden, Australia and Luxembourg) had sailed into the 12-mile Exclusion Zone off Moruroa on the vessel *La Ribaude*. They were apprehended within an hour after entering the zone and towed into the lagoon.

The eight parliamentarians delivered a joint statement to French authorities declaring that France was violating the Nuclear Non-Proliferation Treaty (NPT) and European Atomic Energy Treaty (EURATOM) by resuming its nuclear testing programme. The parliamentarians' joint declaration stated:

> We are united in our demand for an immediate end to nuclear testing at Moruroa. We come in peace and our method of protest is one of complete non-violence. We firmly condemn the arrogance and colonial attitude of the French Government and its indifference and disregard for all the nations of the South Pacific.

The declaration also called on France to release all scientific data on the effects of its nuclear weapons testing and to allow independent scientific investigation. It stated that President Chirac was acting 'in complete contradiction to the whole tradition of France as the cradle of democracy and human rights'.

Manutea also reported that the Greenpeace vessels *Rainbow Warrior* and *MV Greenpeace*, which were seized by the French military, were still being held at Hao Atoll, in French Polynesia. All of the crew had been deported except the skipper of *Rainbow Warrior*, who would not leave his ship.

In the morning we had a 6-foot swordfish on one of the lines, but Dennis and young Paul let it get off. Dennis said he was glad when it got away because 'it was a graceful looking creature with wonderful colours'. Regardless, we had no gaff hook on board – it had been left behind in Wellington. So this became the project for the day: Dennis and Paul made a gaff from a 3-foot piece of pipe and a large stainless steel nail. 'Watch out, next big fish!'

Two flying fish landed on deck; I ate them for brekkie! Dennis and I experimented with baking fresh bread. We had no recipe on board but remembered the general ingredients from way back: flour, water, yeast, milk, oil and salt. I couldn't decide whether one put eggs in or not. It didn't matter because, as far as we could tell, our eggs had never made it on board. Dennis loved eggs and he methodically searched every hole and crevice on the boat looking for them. We had ordered them, paid for them, and the crew remembered seeing them amongst the provisions, but they were nowhere to be found. Dennis was going through withdrawal pains! We made two very big loaves of bread and they came out okay.

The boom gooseneck track came loose so Dennis and I had to re-drill four holes and tap them for larger bolts. We also used the opportunity to straighten the small bit of mainsail track, which was bent when the boom came off its track earlier in the trip. The mainsail was finally in proper operating mode again.

That day we topped our best speed, clocking 16.8 knots when surfing down a huge wave. We were travelling 8 knots, reaching off south-east winds of 25 knots, with large rolling seas. Moruroa was 135 nautical miles away (17 to 20 sailing hours). We were likely to arrive at nightfall the next day.

The water was very warm and the colour had changed from a cold green to a pacific blue. The tops of the waves had turquoise streaks through them. I put on my shorts for the first time and the butter was so soft I could spread it like margarine.

The news of *La Ribaude* entering the Exclusion Zone with Members of Parliament and journalists from a number of different countries boosted our resolve and gave us some assurance that things were happening. It sounded as if the campaign would be more than just a 'float about Moruroa' exercise.

Manutea seemed interested in getting the rest of the fleet in the area to discuss tactics. We began composing our arrival letter to the French Commander at Moruroa.

Chapter 7

Arrival at Moruroa!

On the 10th of September, we arrived at Moruroa! *New Zealand Maid*, *Kela* and *Chimera* arrived 3 hours ahead of us and were greeted just before dark by the New Zealand government research ship *Tui* with cameras blazing. What a welcome by the *Tui*. The ship had a number of journalists and TV crew on board.

I called *Tui* on the radio and informed them of our position. *Tui* came and greeted us before escorting us to the location of the other three Wellington yachts. The *Tui* was the first vessel we had seen since leaving Wellington 20 days previously. It felt good to finally arrive. John Campbell, skipper of *Tui*, informed us of the two letters we were likely to receive from the French Commander. He also said he would supply water for us in the morning and send people around to say hello.

September 11
We were hove-to all night and in the morning set sail to the general meeting area on the north-west part of Moruroa. It was the first time all four boats from Wellington were sailing together. We put on all our flags and banners, and just in time; we were buzzed by a jet plane that made three very low passes, followed by a helicopter. They were taking pictures with very sensitive camera gear. They came so close we could see the cameraman in action peering through some sort of large black tube. We were disturbed by the surveillance and Dennis suggested we give them a 'brown eye'. So three of us dropped our shorts and pointed our very white buttocks skyward towards the helicopter as they manoeuvred in to take pictures. We had a good laugh over this, but the French were not smiling at all.

Vanavana

Tureia

Flotilla meeting location

12 mile exclusion zone

Moruroa

Fangataufa

0   15   30

Nautical miles

The Protest Campaign location

Tui came on the scene and the four Wellington boats lined up to take on fuel and water. *Chimera* went first. The technique used for refuelling at sea required *Tui* to hold a steady course to windward at 2.5 knots. The vessels taking on fuel and water came alongside one at a time, maintaining the same speed and motoring parallel to the *Tui* at a distance of around 7–10 metres. A hose was thrown from the *Tui* and the refuelling began.

Again, the French helicopter flew by and took photographs of the operation at close range while a French frigate continued to circle us at a distance of about a mile. We sensed that they were not happy to see the New Zealand government ship blatantly assisting the protest flotilla. They were careful to fully document the event.

The whole operation gave us a great feeling of solidarity. Here were five Kiwi boats, including the government ship which showed total support like a mother hen. Off our backstay we flew an enormous New Zealand flag loaned to us by Dennis's good friend John Curtis, and we were all proud of it. We couldn't have given the French Government a more obvious show of self discipline and national determination to demonstrate against their bombs!

After *Chimera* finished refuelling, a process that seemed to take forever, *New Zealand Maid* was next, then *Kela* and finally us. We chatted with the *Tui* crew as we tanked up on water. Because we had sailed the whole way from New Zealand, we needed no fuel.

We mentioned to the *Tui* crew that we had lots of kiwifruit on board and they said they wanted some. Young Paul pulled out our huge box of kiwifruit and the show began. He began tossing them to the *Tui* crew about 10 metres away in the rolling sea. Dennis and Giles joined in and about 40 kiwifruit were tossed. That worked out to be one for each of the *Tui* crew. It was a bit of a game, as the crew scrambled to make the catch before the fruit splattered all over their decks. Dennis asked, "Hey, aren't you guys supposed to be throwing us food, not the other way round?" They chuckled. They were all out of fresh food themselves and were planning to steam back to the Cook Islands soon to reprovision and pick up new crew.

It was very difficult to steer a straight course in the seas while taking on water. I was, at one stage, enjoying watching the kiwifruit tossing game rather than concentrating on steering a straight course and we came alarmingly close to crashing into the large research ship. We heard later that one of the earlier New Zealand boats, *Triptych*, did actually smash into the ship, resulting in some structural damage.

Tui sent a tender to *New Zealand Maid* and *Kela* to collect Barbara, Cath and the four younger children for a few hours of ice cream, fish and chips, video games and, of course, to face the TV cameras. Barbara and Cath enjoyed hot showers and a chance to compare notes in relative privacy. Cath, who was not feeling well, took the opportunity to see the ship's doctor. It was reassuring to have *Tui* there; they played their support role magnificently, and we were all happy to see that that role was substantially different from what we expected from the briefing we had before the trip by the New Zealand Assistant Chief of Naval Staff (operations), Bill Rathburn.

The navigator from *Tui* came on board *Joie* and delivered a news pack and a chart of Moruroa and Fangataufa with a hand-drawn estimate of the 12-mile Exclusion Zone. The *Tui* crew had prepared the chart especially for the Peace Flotilla. He told us the Wellington boats made the fastest passage from New Zealand of any of the flotilla yachts, averaging 150 nautical miles per day. He also said there were already four vessels and a score of Zodiac inflatables confiscated by the French military. Two of the vessels were currently in the Moruroa Lagoon. One was a small French yacht named *Kidu*, which we knew nothing about, and the other was *La Ribaude*.

Dennis and I finished drafting our letter to be delivered to the Commander at Moruroa. We would exchange this letter with the two letters we expect to receive from them. It read as follows:

September 11, 1995

Base Commander
Moruroa

Dear Sir,

We, the captain and crew of the yacht *Joie*, wish to make the following statement to yourself, as the representative of the French Government at Moruroa.

We have sailed all the way from New Zealand to represent the views of millions of New Zealanders and to express these views in the form of peaceful protest to your Government.

We believe the people of the world applauded the end of the cold war, bringing relief from the fear of nuclear destruction and a sense of security for future generations.

It was reasonable for ordinary citizens of all nations to expect their leaders to carry this trust forward, working toward and hopefully outlawing these weapons. Indeed the Test Ban Treaty was a step in this direction.

It is not surprising then, that nations and people world-wide have reacted with horror and disbelief at your country's persistence in continuing to test and develop these weapons in line with the cold war attitudes.

It is our personal belief that your actions, and the actions of any nations that continue to develop these weapons, are a crime against the future development of mankind and the other species of this planet.

Your actions are therefore subject to the scrutiny of the international community and your country's laws are superseded by the higher laws governing the well-being of our common and shared environment.

We carry no weapons on board. Again we wish to remind you that we come in peaceful non-violent protest. We would welcome discussions with yourself and your representatives on this matter. We would also ask that you forward this letter to President Chirac and the President of French Polynesia.

Your sincerely,

(Signed by all the crew)

PS: The captain, Lynn Pistoll, is proud that his vessel has a French name *Joie*, short for 'Joie de Vivre' (Joy of Life) and says 'I named my boat after your beautiful French expression and have faith that this aspect of your culture will prevail in the end!'

The other yachts all composed their own letters and worked out how they intended to deal with the French Government and military according to the principles of their own crew members. Jon Tucker from *New Zealand Maid* shared their letter with us. It read as follows:

> To: Commander French Military Forces
> Moruroa/Fangataufa

We, owners and crew of New Zealand registered ship *New Zealand Maid*, wish to inform the French Government through you that:

a) We do not recognise France's right to create and contain nuclear wastes in the Pacific region against the wishes of nearly all Pacific inhabitants.

b) We do not recognise France's right to declare an Exclusion Zone around Moruroa and Fangataufa atolls.

c) In view of the French military's record of violence against peaceful protest we do not intend to endanger our children aboard this vessel by sailing inside the zone.

d) We feel strongly that France has abused its political authority by overriding the wishes of all Pacific nations and creating a long term contamination problem.

e) We are not anti-French, we admire many French citizens especially sailors like Eric Tabarly, Bernard Moitessire and especially Jacques Cousteau. However, uniformed French military personnel are not welcome aboard this boat.

f) We are proving to Jacques Chirac that Moruroa is within easy access to ordinary New Zealand families and is part of New Zealand's 'back yard'.

Signed 10/9/95

Jon Tucker (owner skipper), New Zealander
Barbara Tucker (part owner), New Zealander
Daniel Tucker, New Zealander
Sam Tucker (aged 12 years), New Zealander
Matthew Tucker (aged 10 years), New Zealander
Jim MacArthur, New Zealander
Adriaan Stroess, European citizen

The Wellington boats moved around to the flotilla meeting place: 21° 40′ S, 139° 20′ W, just outside the north-west corner of the 12-mile Exclusion Zone of Moruroa. It was like coming into a small floating village. Six other protest boats had already assembled there. It was a wonderful and highly emotional moment, sailing in among the craft that we had all come to know on the radio waves and with whom we felt a very close bond of allegiance. All around us people cheered and waved, fire-crackers were let off and horns sounded; we had arrived!

We had arrived, but it was a very odd feeling because there was no land in sight. It was like parking in the middle of the ocean. We could not see where Moruroa or Fangataufa Islands were because they were flat, low lying atolls. The sea was not subdued at all by their nearby presence.

Atolls are coral islands, typically consisting of a narrow, horseshoe-shaped reef with a shallow lagoon. They are basically formed when old volcanoes or other bits of land slowly sink over hundreds of years. Coral, which is a living organism, grows to the surface of the immersing island and becomes the basis for the island. The highest points on most atolls are typically the coconut palms, and at sea level these cannot be seen from a distance of 12 nautical miles. The only references we had to help us determine our location were the sun, moon, stars and sea swell. We would have to rely heavily on our GPS to find the exact meeting position and to monitor our distance from the 12-mile Exclusion Zone.

We had arrived but there was no friendly harbour in which to rest, reprovision or recreate. There was no break from the exhausting routine of watch-keeping. We were still at sea, bobbing up and down and having to deal with the variable wind and currents, which ran up to 3 knots at times. Additionally, we had to keep a close eye on the many other boats in the vicinity including the French military. This was not going to be an easy protest. We were already stressed out!

Moruroa lies too far south to be free of the Southern Ocean swells and the area was renowned for what has been labelled the 'Moruroa Roll'. The trade winds cycle from south-east to north-east, and regularly reach 25–30 knots with an uncomfortable cross sea. Even the mighty *R Tucker*

Thompson's towering topmasts disappeared behind the swells on occasion.

What would make matters even more complex for us was the fact that the 12-mile Exclusion Zone was not a neat and clean circle in the ocean, marked by floating buoys and lights. Rather, it was an imaginary line that followed the rough contour of Moruroa. The shape more closely resembled Casper the Friendly Ghost in flight! Adding to the confusion, the French had also drawn an imaginary 12-mile Exclusion Zone around the neighbouring test island of Fangataufa, which was 20 nautical miles south of Moruroa.

Because the two 12-mile exclusion zones converged, there was a 4-mile overlap between the two islands. My chart looked like a lesson in co-ordinate geometry.

Dennis said, "This is like living next to a bloody minefield. Half your mind is always concentrating on where you are because the boat is always moving around, so your mind is saying: where is the damn thing and are we out of it or are we on the edge?"

Oddly, given the importance the French authorities attribute to staying outside the zone, they do not publish a proper chart of the area with the legal 12-mile limit drawn on it. The chart we received from *Tui* had a hand-drawn estimate of the zone. Upon close inspection, it looked to be out by as much as 2 miles in at least one spot. So why hadn't the French authorities provided us with a proper chart? That would have been the respectable thing to do.

Interestingly, it was the 20-mile gap between the two islands of Moruroa and Fangataufa that sparked a legal debate between the Peace Flotilla and the French. Because the exclusion zones of the two islands were greater than the distance between the islands, one could not make passage between them without coming under French military discipline.

At least, this was what the French authorities said. According to maritime law, the United Nations Convention on the Law of the Sea grants an explicit power to suspend passage altogether when deemed essential to the State's security. The Peace Flotilla announced its intention to sail between the islands, arguing that the French Government had no right to impose two 12-mile limits because it was not an issue of national security.

The French Government submitted on numerous occasions that the tests were completely safe. It was ironic that, when it came to the ecological consequences of testing, the tests were completely 'safe', but when it came to peaceful protest, they were 'dangerous'. Surely, the reason for imposing the exclusion zones was to suppress protest, and therefore it was illegal. They had no right to stop the innocent passage of vessels through the strait.

France would certainly be unable to indicate any instances, at least since it went underground, when imposing the zone had been necessary for any purpose other than suppressing protest. Additionally, when *Rainbow Warrior* was boarded and tear-gassed in July, France was not yet nuclear testing. There was no possible reason for the action other than to suppress protest.

Upon hearing of the flotilla's intention to sail between Moruroa and Fangataufa, the French navy delivered new warning letters to each vessel declaring that they would consider this a violation and the offending vessels would be confiscated.

Upon arrival at our new home, Henk Haazen, a Greenpeace activist aboard *Vega*, came to greet us in a Zodiac. Henk was a big and strong man in his late thirties with long blond hair and a strong Dutch accent. He reminded me of a Viking. He drove the Zodiac with great skill and one could tell by his actions that he was a very experienced seaman.

He came to pick up Dennis and me for a general meeting aboard the *R Tucker Thompson*. The *Tucker Thompson*, as she was soon to be called, looked like a grand old sailing vessel. It was actually a relatively new vessel but designed as a classical square-rigged schooner, about 85 feet long. When we arrived, we met the infamous David McTaggart, who first sailed *Vega* to Moruroa in 1972 in a protest against French open air atmospheric tests. He also protested at Moruroa in 1973, 1981, 1982 and 1985, and was a true veteran of these waters. He was a founder and prominent leader of Greenpeace. McTaggart welcomed the new arrivals from Wellington and chided us for breaking his previous 21-day record sail to Moruroa by one day!

Also present at the meeting were the skippers of the other nine yachts. One boat, *Bebinka*, came all the way from Chile, sailed single-handedly by her skipper Elan; a very interesting character. Six of the boats were from New Zealand. Two Kiwi boats had already left Moruroa (*Triptych* and *Aquila d'Oro*), and another six were still on their way.

The meeting was very informal. It was led by John Simpson, skipper of the New Zealand boat *Photina*. David McTaggart, although appearing a bit frail, was a real natural in the discussions and was instrumental at driving the key issues. With glittering light blue eyes he said, "If anyone can spare rubber dinghies or if any boat is prepared to 'go in', then you should talk to me personally." He revealed plans to send two Tahitians into the zone on a vaka (traditional Polynesian outrigger canoe) and mentioned another plan that he was reluctant to elaborate on at the time.

Audrey Cardwell, from the 112-foot chartered *Manutea* and who was the official Greenpeace campaign co-ordinator for the protest, briefed us on the latest world developments, including a UN resolution asking France to stop all tests and to release all scientific information for examination.

Because *Tui* was going back to Rarotonga for reprovisioning the following day, they asked for all six New Zealand boats to line up under sail for a television camera shoot. The skippers decided at the meeting to use this event to initiate our first action in the protest campaign.

The *Tucker Thompson* crew invited us back on board for a barbecue later that evening. It was reasonably rough, with 20-knot winds blowing in the open ocean, but we all managed to clamber on board. Giles brought a bottle of rum. I hove *Joie* to windward, abandoned her, and went to the party. I met some interesting Greenpeace people there, but was there for less than an hour when I noticed *Joie* slowly sailing by the heavier *Tucker Thompson*, on a possible collision course with *Manutea*. I asked Roger, one of the people at the barbie, to give me a lift over in the rubber Zodiac. I spent the rest of the evening on board *Joie*, looking after her course while my crew partied on.

After my crew returned we began motoring away from

the flotilla to heave-to at a safer distance where there was more sea room. Before we could clear the flotilla, I heard the familiar sound of the engine speeding up, then dying completely. I knew we had air in the diesel line somewhere. As it was very late and dark, we sailed out of the flotilla pack and would wait until the morning to fix the fuel problem.

The next morning we discovered we had drifted 8 miles downwind from the meeting location. I was anxious to get the engine going again should we need it to get back on location. We removed stowage from the engine room to access the engine. Upon blowing pressure into the main fuel tank, diesel spurted out at a great rate from a crack in the fuel line. We had obviously damaged it when we removed the tank to repair the propeller shaft earlier. We had to bleed the whole system, including the filters, to get the engine going again.

On our way back to location, a French patrol boat moved to within 300 metres of us. We saw a flurry of activity on the back of the vessel where a group of sailors were preparing to launch their inflatable. Before long, it was in the water and four commandos were speeding their way towards us. 'What are they up to?' we wondered. Because we were currently separated from the rest of the flotilla, we were sitting ducks. 'Would the French attack us in international waters?' We hoped that they were only coming over to deliver the two letters we were expecting from the Admiral.

As they got closer, we could see with the binoculars that one of the men was holding a brown envelope in his hand. They came alongside, and with very serious demeanour and a heavy accent, one of the French commandos asked, "We have two letters to deliver to your captain from the Admiral. Will you accept them?"

We had been waiting for this moment for some time and had discussed how we would handle the situation. I said, "I am the Captain, and will accept the letters on two conditions: first, you must accept our letter to your Admiral and President Chirac." Dennis butted in at this stage and said, "and secondly, we would like your permission to take pictures of you, because YOU represent France and YOU are responsible for this atrocity against mankind, and YOU four people in this Zodiac, as crew of that French Patrol boat over there, are a part of it and must claim personal responsibility for this shameful act. We would like to take pictures of you to show our children back home who the real people are behind this all."

Well, this took them by total surprise. They were relatively young guys and did not know how to handle it. The leader called back to the ship on his hand held radio asking for permission for us to take pictures of them. I did not wait for the answer, and started blazing away with my camera. They were very ashamed and looked away when I asked them to face the camera. We exchanged letters and they high-tailed their way back to their ship.

I suppose it was easy to do bad things for your country when you personally were not regarded as the wrongdoer. But the action of these young French guys showed that when confronted by their own conscience, they were ashamed.

We opened the brown envelope to find two letters inside. The first letter read:

Forces Maritimes   Papeete Le 24/8/95
Et Zone Maritime Du Pacifique

L'Amiral

Le Skipper,

You came, with your crew, to protest by your presence on board a sailing ship in the vicinity of the Mururoa atoll against the decision made by France to carry out a final series of 8 nuclear tests, due to end by 31 May 1996 latest, prior to signing the Nuclear Test Ban Treaty in 1996.

Naturally, I do not share your point of view, although you should know that I respect it. As long as your ship will remain on the high seas, no objection can be raised to your demonstration.

On the other hand, as you are a seasoned sailor, you must be acquainted with the rules of international maritime law pertaining to the right of passage of ships in territorial waters of a country whose flag they do not

fly, and you must surely be aware that a coastal State has
– pursuant to Article 25 of the United Nations
Convention on the Law of the Sea (which reflects the
common law pertaining to this issue) – the right to
suspend locally, in specified areas of its territorial sea,
the exercising of the right of innocent passage.

By the order n° 707 of 23 June 1995, the High
Commissioner of the Republic in French Polynesia has
suspended until 31 May 1996 the right of innocent
passage in the territorial waters bordering the Mururoa
and Fangataufa atolls. This measure is in conformity
with international law.

If you contravene this prohibition, you will be
liable to prosecution under French law which, as you
know, is sovereign in this area.

The right of passage to which you are entitled in
the rest of the French territorial sea in Polynesia must
therefore be exercised in accordance with international
law and French regulations pertaining to defence issues
and to coastal security. Any infringement of French
regulations will entail criminal prosecution.

As a sailor, I have spent a great part of my life at
sea, partly in the Pacific, and I know that conditions can
often be tough there. I assure you that I shall always
react as a sailor should you encounter difficulties and
that I would not hesitate to lend you assistance if
necessary, but please also bear in mind that I am quite
determined to enforce the law and to carry out the
mission I hold to safeguard the security of the testing
sites in order to implement the decisions made by the
President of the French Republic.

Sincerely,
Vice-admiral Philippe EUVERTE

Well, we thought that last paragraph was a charming
touch of French chivalry anyway. The second letter was in
response to the flotilla claiming the right to be able to make
innocent passage under international law between the islands
of Moruroa and Fangataufa. It read as follows:

COMMANDEMENT SUPERIEUR DES
FORCES ARMEES DE LA POLYNESIE
FRANCAISE

L'AMIRAL
TO ALL SKIPPERS
OF THE PROTEST FLOTILLA VESSELS

I remind you that Arrête N° 707 of 23 June, 1995 has suspended the right of innocent passage in the territorial sea surrounding the atolls of Fangataufa and Moruroa, as it is allowed by article 25 of the Montego Bay Convention on the Law of the Sea.

The Territorial sea between Fangataufa and Moruroa is only an optional and not a necessary itinerary. This zone therefore does not stand for a strait permitting international navigation allowing to the Montego Bay Convention.

The right that you claim to exercise from today at noon can not in any case be accepted. If you still persist, I will enforce the law: you will expose your crews to be questioned and your vessels taken under our control.

Sincerely, Vice-admiral Philippe EUVERTE

The 4th of September, 1995

CHAPTER 8

Campaign Activities

After reading with interest the two French letters warning us to be good little boys, we motor-sailed back to the general meeting location for the planned TV shoot. It took about an hour for the six New Zealand boats to manoeuvre into position. *Tui* then sailed by at close range, coming straight at us with TV cameras blazing.

We luffed our sails to slow up our speed and stayed in second place behind the slower *Tucker Thompson*, which was leading the pack. As soon as the TV shoot was over, we hardened in the sails and went for the line as planned. *Joie* took the lead position and the other yachts followed. We could see large puffs of smoke billowing from the French patrol boat and the large frigate monitoring our activities nearby. They knew we were up to something and were steaming full speed toward us.

By my calculations we were on the line or perhaps slightly inside the 12-mile Exclusion Zone. The Navy boat veered closely in front of us. Nick, who was further behind, called us on the SSB radio and said we had a warning from the French military on VHF channel 16. Our VHF radio had broken only the day before, when we were talking to *Tui*. Nick said they asked us to 'state our intentions, and to change course back out of the zone'. I reminded Nick that our VHF radio was broken and asked him to tell the French to broadcast their warning to me on SSB channel 4417. This did not happen. Afterwards, I realised that SSB was a long-distance transmission. If the French had used it, they would have broadcast their warning to the world!

We were all electrified, especially Dennis, who was grinning from ear to ear, and experiencing a major adrenaline rush. I got a little nervous about what the French military might do next, so we quickly tacked and headed back out in the opposite direction. The French patrol boat seemed satisfied with our course change, then headed towards *Photina*, which had just entered the zone further west.

As the patrol vessel approached *Photina*, we reversed tack and again headed toward the zone. *Photina* tacked back out in the nick of time. The patrol boat then again sped towards us at full speed. Once she got close we tacked back out to sea again. *New Zealand Maid* and *Chimera* also joined in, and we had the dead serious French Navy Patrol vessel running around in circles at full steam.

This cat-and-mouse game continued for about 15–20 minutes before the New Zealand boats retired. Dennis said, "I haven't had so much fun since mum caught her tit in the wringer!" The French obviously did not share in our jubilation; they looked very pissed off. We could clearly see the grim expressions on their faces when they came close. No-one was smiling!

We were all elated and satisfied with our first encounter with the French military. We tested them at the line and we had survived. But if *Tui* had not been on location, ready to film any likely attack upon us, we could not have been sure what the French might have done. They certainly had a history of aggression to protect their testing programme.

Moruroa, in the native Polynesian language of Maohi, means the Place of the Great Secret. This is a cruelly appropriate name for a once-beautiful palm-covered atoll in the Tuamotu Islands of French Polynesia. France had conducted some 187 nuclear tests at Moruroa and nearby Fangataufa atolls. Despite world-wide outrage and condemnation, the French Government had exploded the first in a new round of tests just one week before we arrived.

The French Government themselves helped lay the foundation for the growth of the Greenpeace organisation. Although Greenpeace was originally founded in 1971 to oppose US nuclear testing off the coast of Alaska, it really developed strength owing to the French atmospheric testing in 1972 and 1973, when David McTaggart protested at Moruroa aboard his 38-foot ketch *Vega*. *Vega* was back at

Moruroa again, and it was a pleasure seeing this famous sailing vessel. What a protest history this small boat has had; she had been to Moruroa several times and had even sailed to Vladivostok.

In 1985 the French Government, fearing the attention that Greenpeace would bring to its tests, bombed and sank the *Rainbow Warrior* in Auckland, New Zealand. Greenpeace crew member Fernando Pereira was killed in the bombing. I still vividly remember the day it happened. I was on the Wellington motorway driving to work and an announcement came over the radio that a bombing had occurred and *Rainbow Warrior* had been sunk.

Later it was discovered that the French Government had done the dirty deed! How unbelievable it was. France had committed state terrorism and murder in a foreign country. Yet, they managed to walk away from the horrendous crime with minimal repercussion and eventually honoured the murderers as heroes back in France.

The animosity that exists between Greenpeace and the French military was understandable and once again they were in a confrontational situation. While we were still en route to Moruroa, French forces moved early to confiscate the two Greenpeace vessels and stifle the protest campaign. We learned from Greenpeace crew the details of what happened:

At 5.30 a.m. on September 1, Greenpeace launched an all-out assault on the atoll. Nine inflatable boats and a helicopter carried 22 Greenpeace activists into Moruroa lagoon. Moments later *Rainbow Warrior* crossed into the Exclusion Zone heading for the test site. Two divers jumped out of the inflatables and positioned themselves under a test monitoring barge.

The French military response was swift. Activists were arrested in the lagoon by French commandos carrying spears to puncture the inflatable boats. On *Rainbow Warrior*, US Congressman Eni Faleomavaega (American Samoa), Oscar Temaru, leader of the Tahitian independence movement and the ship's crew were arrested after commandos broke through welded hatches and reinforced windows to stop the ship's progress toward Moruroa. When Greenpeace's helicopter returned to the *MV Greenpeace* in international waters, French commandos boarded and seized that vessel too.

Commandos spray-painted the windows and destroyed communications equipment on both vessels, cutting whole lengths from cables and spraying a glue-like substance into the computers. They then used sledgehammers, blowtorches and powered cutting equipment to smash doors and windows. A skeleton crew was forcibly separated on the *MV Greenpeace* in an incident involving violence and injuries.

Although most of the Greenpeace resistance was passive, we heard of some violent scuffles. One man was carried away and a legionnaire kicked him in the head. Others were punched and some were dragged up the stairs with their heads banging on the steps. Greenpeace said that protesters had been punched and dragged, handcuffed, along coral. Greenpeace crew retaliated by ripping the teargas masks off commandos and throwing them overboard. They also threw any equipment put down by commandos overboard. John Castle, the *Rainbow Warrior* captain, hid up in the crow's nest with a hand-held radio for 30 hours before being discovered by the commandos.

The helicopter was lifted off the *MV Greenpeace* at Moruroa and then both vessels were towed to the island of Hao, about 280 miles north-west of Moruroa. All of the crew were eventually released, except Stephanie Mills (campaign co-ordinator), the *MV Greenpeace* captain and two others. These four people, after being held at Hao Island for 6 days, were flown to Paris against their will and subsequently expelled from France.

How could the French military do this and get away with it? Clearly this was a disproportionate and unreasonable response. In the event of an infraction by a helicopter or inflatable, what right did France have to confiscate an entire vessel, use excessive force against and restrain the crew, loot their personal property and destroy communication equipment? What right did France have to tow the vessels to a remote island far away from the scene and hold them indefinitely? The Greenpeace vessels did not have any weapons and were not attacking. The French did not claim to be acting in self-defence. They did not even lay criminal charges against the crew or vessels.

The French authorities allowed Greenpeace campaign co-ordinator Stephanie Mills to transmit a letter to her family after being detained for nearly 4 days. Stephanie's slightly adapted letter read:

My dear family,
We have been detained illegally and against our will on board *Rainbow Warrior* for 84 hours. We have been forbidden to communicate and are not allowed access to the local radio, onto the bridge, or into the machine room. All communication equipment has been either disconnected or broken, and the engines have been damaged. We are being towed near Hao.

We have been told that we are 'free' but that if we do not obey the officers they are authorised to use military force against us. There are 12 to 15 paratroopers on board. The French authorities have allowed us to send a message to our lawyer via military radio. This letter will be first transmitted and read by Admiral Euverte, according to the gendarmes.

Last Sunday, I was assaulted by two commandos when I tried to take a photograph. I was thrown on the ground and the camera was thrown overboard. I have some bruises but I am all right. Our forced detention is as illegal as the nuclear testing. We are protesting and will go on protesting at our imprisonment and about the tests. We are asking to see our lawyer immediately and seek all legal means to prove our democratic right to protest in a peaceful non-violent way and we have the intention to exercise our rights against those that detain us illegally. Please call on our behalf the families of the crew. They have been fantastic.

Love to all of you. I know that you are thinking about me like I am thinking about you. I couldn't do it without you. Send my love to Michael.
Arohanui, Stephanie.

PS They have told me that this letter will not be censored.

Fortunately, the Greenpeace-leased vessel S/V *Manutea*, already under way to Moruroa, arrived the following day to continue with the campaign and to support the private peace flotilla, which was growing in number.

Governments around the world stepped up their protest with the news of the confiscation of the two Greenpeace vessels and of France's first test, which followed shortly after. Chile and New Zealand recalled their ambassadors from France; the Japanese and Australian Governments lodged strong protests; the South Pacific Forum called the action 'inexcusable and provocative'; Indonesia was unhappy and would be sending a protest statement; and the Clinton administration and Russia expressed their 'regrets'. In France, 5000 people staged a protest in Paris. Although the governments of China and Britain refrained from officially denouncing the tests, pubic opinion in Britain was strongly against the French action; and one would have to question whether the Chinese public even knew the tests were taking place.

In France an opinion poll on the eve of the first test showed that 63 percent of French people opposed the tests and only 29 percent were in favour. Chirac had faced the largest fall in popularity of any president in modern French history since taking office in May 1995. The country's scientific community also lent its weight, with about 1300 French scientists joining some 1100 foreign counterparts in signing a petition calling on Chirac to abandon the programme.

Within 12 hours of the blast, the European Commission voted to ask France to provide more information on the impact of testing before any further tests. This was requested under Article 34 of the EURATOM Treaty (European Atomic Energy Community). The EURATOM Treaty is one of the founding treaties of the European Community signed in 1957.

Article 34 of the treaty obliges a country to give the European Commission information on the additional health and safety measures in place for 'particularly dangerous experiments', and obliges the Commission to render its opinion on these measures before such experiments were carried out. The treaty recognises the Commission's prior approval where the effects of such experiments were likely to affect the territories of other member states. In this case, the territory of nearby Pitcairn Island (UK), could be considered 'a member state'.

Under the article, the Commission had the right to inspect nuclear facilities to verify the operation and efficiency of their monitoring of radioactivity levels in the air, water and soil, and to ensure compliance with basic health and safety standards to protect the health of workers and the general public.

Spontaneous boycotts of French products erupted around the world and later the US Senate passed a bipartisan resolution condemning the tests.

Yet Chirac still pressed on. It is understandable why, in France, he was nicknamed 'Bulldozer'. His next plan was to offer an 'olive branch' to the European Union by 'Europeanising' France's nuclear weapons. He proposed a common European defence policy based on the French nuclear deterrent. Fortunately, the offer was rejected by the EU Foreign Ministers meeting in Spain, with the exception of the UK, for obvious reasons.

It had been very tense in Tahiti since France announced the resumption of testing. The first nuclear detonation was the straw that broke the camel's back. When we were approaching Moruroa we heard via the SSB radio that there was rioting in Papeete. At the time, we did not appreciate the extent of events which took place.

About 2000 Tahitian anti-nuclear and pro-independence protesters pushed riot police violently aside and torched the international airport terminal. They attacked the residence and offices of the high commissioner of French Polynesia and looted and burned shops. Forty French legionnaires and 300 paramilitary gendarmes were flown to Tahiti from Moruroa and France to quell the situation.

The rioters drove an earth-mover through glass doors at the airport before setting fire to the international and domestic terminals, surrounding palm trees, a nearby bar and more than a dozen cars. They drove the mover around inside the terminal, breaking down internal walls. Aircraft were also damaged as protesters clashed with riot police who were firing teargas canisters, stun grenades and rubber bullets. After sunset, hundreds of protesters marched downtown, smashing windows, looting shops and setting many buildings on fire, including the power station.

Millions of dollars' worth of damage was done. One hundred and thirty cars and 17 buildings were firebombed. Airline schedules were disrupted. Numerous people were injured, and over 100 people were left homeless. Did this really happen in the fun-loving and peaceful South Pacific paradise of Tahiti?

French Polynesian President Gaston Flosse was quick to blame Greenpeace and New Zealand and Australian politicians for helping to incite the riots by participating in protest marches in Papeete and giving their seal of approval to everything that happened. French officials then went on a persecution trail, asking television crews and photographers to surrender film of the riots. They used this and other information to convict people. It was reported that 237 people were jailed on riot-related charges, some receiving 4-month jail terms.

We had another general meeting of skippers and Greenpeace activists on *Tucker Thompson*. New actions were proposed.

Dennis suggested that each of the flotilla vessels could make one or two floating radar reflectors. They could be made out of cardboard, old egg cartons, aluminium foil or what ever was available. The idea was to launch these floating radar reflectors into the zone from many different locations. The French would pick them up on their radar screens and be obliged to investigate. This would keep them totally busy and confused. Someone suggested that a radar reflector could be made from wrapping aluminium foil around a balloon, but no one had any balloons.

At this point Russell Harris, skipper of the *Tucker Thompson*, said, "Wait a minute", and disappeared aft. He reappeared shortly with a gross of condoms! As his crew were of mixed gender, he considered condoms part of the ship's basic supplies. He passed several around and people began blowing them up. We all laughed and collapsed in hysterics!

We made a few prototypes and launched them nearby to

test the signal strength using the flotilla's radar. Unfortunately, they were too small and too close to the water to be distinguished from a wave. We would have to get the 'balloons' higher off the water and make them bigger. We abandoned the idea because it would have required helium, which no one had.

We focused on the next proposed action. This plan was for two Tahitian men to paddle a vaka into Moruroa.

It was not clear exactly how these men got to Moruroa, but they probably had been smuggled out in one of the boats from Papeete. They were dressed in traditional Tahitian clothing and wore long hair braided in a number of lines stemming from the centre of their heads, Rastafarian style. They were from an anti-nuclear organisation in Tahiti called Hiti Tau.

They spoke only Tahitian and French, so one of the crew translated for them. They explained that the grandmother of one of the Tahitians was born on Moruroa and the other man worked there for 10 years during the French testing programme. They were very emotional about the action they were about to do. They spoke in reverence, in single sentences, and waited for the translator to relay their message in English. They said that the French Government came and took their land without permission, and paid nothing for it. They would paddle to Moruroa in the vaka to claim their land back.

This was no easy task. They had to paddle in an open canoe through 12 miles of ocean, through potentially large seas, with a high risk of being swamped.

The plan was to transfer the vaka from *Tucker Thompson* to *Vega* early in the morning. At daybreak (5 a.m.) all the boats would go towards the line and *Vega* would release the vaka. The other boats would huddle around *Vega* to prevent it from being seized by the French military.

The French military claimed that they had the right to seize any vessel in international waters if they could show that an infringing inflatable or other craft was launched from it. Therefore, gathering around the vessel from which an action was launched became one of the most important roles of the Peace Flotilla. We acted like a smoke screen. The French could not ascertain which vessel launched the infringing craft, and the captured protesters were sworn to secrecy.

The plan worked well and the two Tahitians began paddling away from the nest of the flotilla towards Moruroa. At that moment, two very large humpback whales heralded their departure, symbolically breaching out of the water several times. They breached right next to *Vega* and other Peace Flotilla boats without any fear of our presence. I was very surprised to see whales in the warm water of the South Pacific and wondered if it was typical for them to be there. Later, the Tahitians said they knew the whales would be there. This was part of Polynesian folklore and their presence was a good omen.

The French patrol boat realised we were up to something and steamed full ahead. Henk, from *Vega*, followed the vaka in a Zodiac for a mile or so to make sure they would not be mistreated or even 'done in' by the French military once they were caught. He then raced full-speed back to the flotilla.

The Tahitians paddled on and were soon out of sight. The Navy patrol boat eventually spotted them but let them continue paddling. They obviously did not know how to handle the situation of two local Polynesians paddling in a traditional vaka to Moruroa to claim their homeland back.

We did not know what happened to them and waited in suspense until the next day. We learnt that they were allowed to paddle into the zone 8 miles before being picked up by the French. Their canoe was actually swamped by the huge seas. They were sent back to Papeete and released without any charges.

The French authorities were obviously very sensitive to any action that involved local Tahitians, fearing that any mistreatment of them would incite further riots. This was their weakness and David McTaggart and Greenpeace knew it.

Dennis and I approached David McTaggart after the next meeting and asked him if we could help in a bigger way. Dennis and I had had a long talk about it, and we felt that since we had come all this distance, we may as well get stuck in a more serious manner.

McTaggart was pleased with our offer and he invited us aboard *Manutea* for further discussions. We had a few beers and he told us the episode of *La Ribaude* when she was confiscated earlier in the campaign. "We were lucky the French came out and got 'em," he laughed. "We brought the Parliamentarians and journalists out on *Machias* then transferred them to *La Ribaude*. The weather wasn't very good; it was a near gale and there were 2-metre swells. Most of them were desk-bound politicians and had little experience with the sea. The dinghy transfer was real frightening for them; they were wretchedly seasick and got wet and cold.

"The boat was in real bad shape; the engine was stuffed. It was blowing quite hard and we sent them in there. *La Ribaude* couldn't hold course against the strong wind and it would have been blown right back out of the Exclusion Zone. Thank God, the French picked 'em up. The action could have been a real disaster," McTaggart laughed cynically.

He then told us the exciting action conducted by Greenpeace activists Alan Baker and Matthew Whiting before we had arrived. They sailed out on *La Ribaude* when she first arrived then went into Moruroa lagoon on a couple of kayaks. Once in the lagoon, Alan set off a number of flares to distract the French before giving himself up.

Alan was not hurt, but Matthew, who had been chased then finally caught after he had tagged buildings with Greenpeace stickers, was beaten by furious soldiers. While held at gun-point he was hog-tied with a connecting rope around his neck. They swung him around from the tied ropes and dragged him along the ground. One of the soldiers used the butt of his gun to smash Matthew's elbow and knee then he put the muzzle to his head threatening to kill him if he didn't talk. At the base infirmary Matthew received four stitches to the elbow, iodine to the rope burns on his neck and his knee was x-rayed, revealing a fracture.

Both activists were held at Moruroa at the time of the first test, a 20-kilotonne explosion. They reported that the bomb personnel all went to safety platforms in case the explosion caused a tidal wave, or the atoll to sink; but they were left in their cells. At the time of the detonation they were literally raised off the floor. "The floor appeared to drop and then come up and then drop again", McTaggart explained. It's hard to see how solid rock can do this without cracking somewhere.

After a couple more beers, McTaggart reminisced on some of his past adventures with the French bomb administrators. In 1972, when on *Vega*, he had discovered how the French conducted their atmospheric tests. The predominant winds in the area are the south-east trade winds, which blow 80 percent of the time in the direction of Tahiti and other South Pacific Islands countries. But occasionally the wind shifts to the north sector. This was when the French would detonate their devices, because it meant that the fallout would be blown south into the open Pacific Ocean and towards South America.

To make sure the wind patterns were correct, especially at the higher altitudes, the French would launch a meteorological balloon. McTaggart would watch for this weather balloon. When he saw it, he would go to the downwind side of the island and heave-to, thus preventing the French from exploding their open air nuclear devices. Each time he delayed the test, it cost millions of dollars and they would have to wait again until the wind was favourable. Needless to say, McTaggart was not a very popular man with the French bomb administrators. To get him out of the way the military eventually rammed his boat in international waters then towed her into Moruroa lagoon.

He also told us of the 1973 protest in which he was severely beaten by French military officers who boarded *Vega*. He nearly lost an eye in the beating and the French made up some story that he hurt himself when he fell on his boat. His girlfriend took pictures of the incident and smuggled out the film in her vagina. The pictures proved that French officers had beaten him and the story made international news. During these tests he and his crew were often the only protesters and they had no resources for a concerted campaign.

McTaggart felt that the current situation was similar. With the earlier confiscation of the two large Greenpeace vessels, the present protest flotilla had no power against the large French warships. "All we can do is to continue to annoy and frustrate them," he said.

And it was working. After the Tahitian men in the vaka were sent in, the French military came out in full force in a mock raid on the nine flotilla boats. First, a jet plane screamed down deliberately 'dive bombing' each individual boat and tearing across the mastheads at very low altitudes. Then a French helicopter carried on the act of international terrorism.

Meanwhile, the flotilla was outside the 12-mile zone, technically protected by international maritime law. The helicopter buzzed each individual boat, hovering above or whirling around the small vessels and pointing cameras at them. The large French frigates and patrol boats then took their turn, cruising around and through the flotilla like large grey sharks. Without reason they would sometimes turn and sail within metres of the boats. This raid went on continuously for about 2 hours before they were satisfied with their retaliation and returned to their base.

The down-draft from the helicopter was quite dangerous for small sailing boats and Elan, the Chilean single-hander on *Bebinka*, had to radio a protest when his boat was badly knocked down onto her beam ends by the helicopter gust.

I think that Greenpeace made a fundamental strategic error early in the campaign when it lost *Rainbow Warrior* and their flagship *MV Greenpeace* to the French. These vessels, especially the *MV Greenpeace*, carried lots of equipment for an extended campaign, including 'flying Zodiacs', a fast helicopter and sophisticated communications equipment. If they had waited until the rest of the flotilla arrived, they would have been able to deploy their equipment and implement further strategies under the camouflage of the other protest yachts.

This loss severely constrained Greenpeace's ability to shape media perceptions from the test site itself. The remaining Greenpeace ships, *Vega* and *Manutea*, were sailing ships and undeniably inferior in terms of vitality and communications equipment. Greenpeace no longer could beam news videos from the site. The only images came from journalists on the French frigates. This was a significant French coup, and I doubted they would release the Greenpeace vessels until the testing was over.

The civilian Peace Flotilla had been left to carry on with the imagery of resistance, but we had little to work with; only our own small vessels and a few rubber dinghies. Without current film footage and journalists to report our actions, it was unlikely that sending one tiny dinghy after another into the zone would keep the protest in the headlines.

We told McTaggart that we were prepared to sacrifice *Joie* in an action if we could justify the action as a worthy deed. None of the other civilian flotilla boats offered such a sacrifice and McTaggart was tickled pink. So the planning began for what would be our final action: 'The Tureian Claim-Back of Moruroa and Fangataufa'. We planned to do it in about a week or so.

The strangest feeling descended upon me. It was like standing in front of a judge for deliberation and being given the death sentence. I could not believe I made this commitment. I had just offered to give my boat up to the French. Was I nuts? This was the boat that I built and had owned for 20 years. Two of my children were born on her and she was my current home. Gee, I felt sick! I might never get her back again, and if I did, in what condition would she be?

McTaggart was a mover and a shaker and very good at getting things going. He was a strong-willed person, yet he had very good people skills. He sensed the uncertainty in me and tried to alleviate my fears by explaining what was likely to happen. He walked us through the typical arrest procedure.

First, once we were headed towards Moruroa and obviously inside the 12-mile zone, the French military would give us three warnings by radio asking us to state our intentions and to turn around. Second, commandos would board us and take over control of *Joie*. These were specially trained forces dressed in black who do not necessarily carry arms but were equipped with batons and teargas. Finally, we would be taken into Moruroa lagoon and processed by the Gendarmerie Maritime (Marine Police). This would include individual interrogation, photographing and fingerprinting. All the time we would be guarded by French Foreign Legionnaires and other military personnel.

He then ran us through possible penalties. These included: deportation from French Polynesia by air from Moruroa to Tahiti, then on to New Zealand on the first available flight; exclusion orders on our re-entry into Tahiti for 5–10 or more years (this could include us personally and our vessel); and the confiscation of *Joie*.

He said that the charges and penalties we could face were not totally predictable. The military would take us through a 'procès verbale' or questioning on Moruroa, and then pass our case on to the civilian Procurator Generale in Tahiti. It was then up to him and the civilian courts to decide what charges would be brought. Political and other considerations could enter into this deliberation.

McTaggart did say that, in practice, the French authorities were likely to deal with any members of the Peace Flotilla with velvet gloves, at least as long as the eyes of the media were on Moruroa. Even with the confiscation of both *Rainbow Warrior* and *MV Greenpeace* and the number of Zodiac actions already conducted in this campaign, no one had yet been charged by French authorities.

McTaggart also assured us that we would eventually get *Joie* back. He always got *Vega* back, but it required a long and expensive legal process. He offered the services of Greenpeace to assist with legal aid and other financial costs. This was assuring, but I still felt funny about the commitment we had made. The only positive thing about it was that we would get an aeroplane ride back home pretty soon!

Dennis and I took a new idea to the next daily meeting. McTaggart liked it, but the other skippers were a bit reluctant as it involved a lot of sailing and they seemed content just to stay in one general area. We argued that by remaining close together in one area, we were making it very easy for the French military to monitor and harass us. If we spread out around the atoll, we would tax the French resources to cover the entire fleet.

We agreed upon the 'dispersal action'. We were assigned five different locations around the atoll (two boats at each location for mutual protection). At 7 a.m. we would all begin talking on VHF channel 16 in 'secret hype language', then proceed to the 12-mile line at full speed at each of the locations, stopping just short of the line. We would do this again at dusk and the next morning. At each location we would record the details (time, name, number) of French vessels and aircraft that covered the locations. We would then compare the notes and estimate their exact navy resources and weaknesses.

We shared location with *Chimera* at the eastern 'cleavage' of the zone, which was between Moruroa and Fangataufa atolls.

All the boats set sail immediately after the meeting, proceeding in different directions. The French military could not figure out what we were up to, but realised something was going down. The afternoon provided ideal sailing conditions: light winds and gentle seas. It felt good to be sailing again! We planned a course across the northern part of the Exclusion Zone, then south to our location. We expected the trip to take 10–12 hours, which would put us at location around dawn.

We were sailing along comfortably and quite relaxed. Suddenly, Dennis noticed a patrol boat steaming toward us at great speed. He asked me whether I was sure that we were outside the zone. I said yes, of course, but did so with reservation. Because there were no land references, one could never be sure without checking the GPS; we had not checked it for at least 2 hours. I quickly turned on the GPS, got a position and plotted it on the chart. We were indeed inside the zone, by nearly 2 miles! There must have been a strong northerly current setting towards Moruroa, which we were unaware of.

I turned on the hand-held VHF radio, which we had borrowed from *Manutea*. We could hear a Frenchman speaking to us in English, with a strong and stern French accent. He said, "*Joie, Joie*, this is the seventh time in 2 days that you have been inside the 12-mile Exclusion Zone. Please state your intentions, and change course immediately to 030° N." "Oh hell!" I said. "Let's turn this donkey around, and get out of here!" The crew all jumped to their stations and we tacked back out to sea as enthusiastically as if we were rounding a buoy in the America's Cup race.

'Seven times. Wow, have we been that bad already?' I thought to myself. I called the Frenchman up and explained. "The French boat, the French boat, this is the *Joie*. Sorry about that. We were only having a pleasant day sail, and did not know we had drifted into the zone. We will try to pay better attention to our navigation in the future. *Joie* out." They bought it. We were let off the hook one more time! We kept sailing north out of the zone as fast as we could.

We sailed all night to arrive at location, 75 miles from our normal meeting place. At 4 a.m. I called *Chimera* on channel 16: "*Chimera*, code 15 please confirm initiation." Gary returned the call and said, "We're going in." We proceeded towards the line as the night turned into dawn. We looked eagerly for a warship and were confused by the red lights at the entrance to Moruroa; we thought they might be the lights of a frigate. We hove-to at the line and 10 minutes later a warship arrived. She came towards us, but not very close. She must have been satisfied that we were out of the zone and continued sailing westward through the pass between the two islands.

We learnt a couple of things from this exercise. First, it became apparent that the French had only limited boats to cover us all if we spread around the atoll. Secondly, they appeared to consider us of little threat at the south-east part of the atoll and let us be. Entering Moruroa in a rubber inflatable from this side could be fatal; protesters would have to pass over the perilous fringing coral reef with breaking seas. At this location, the French did not even bother to buzz us by plane or helicopter.

We caught two tuna, gave half of one to *Chimera* and ate the rest. They were well received as we had not had fresh protein for a while. We joked about their potential radioactivity and how we would begin glowing after eating them. However, we took our chances and ravaged them hoping that all of the French talk about the safety of the surrounding environment was not just propaganda! At least we knew that tuna were a long-distance migratory species, not like the reef fish in the lagoon. The tuna were delicious and boosted our energy levels.

September 18

It took two full days to complete the 'dispersal action'. On our return to the meeting location we re-gathered for a debriefing. The skippers reported very little French military coverage from remote areas around the atoll. McTaggart was very excited about the findings and keen to do it again, but this time he wanted to send an inflatable with four activists into the zone from one of the distant locations. We all agreed to the plan, but some reluctantly, as sailing was much more demanding than heaving-to all day. This meant resumption of watches, sleepless nights, getting wet and cold, and the other inconveniences of passage making. Ours was the lucky boat this time; *Joie* was chosen to stay at the meeting location.

After the meeting we exchanged crew in quite rough seas. Henk was the chauffeur. He was very skilled at handling the Zodiac in those conditions. He would approach a boat at full speed, then cut the engine just in time to gently plough into the side of the boat, which would be bobbing up and down in the deep swells. He then yelled instructions to the waiting passengers to jump in. Doing so was always a bit scary. One had to calculate the jump to leave the boat when the Zodiac was at the top of a crest, and the yacht was at the bottom of it. Otherwise, there was a 6-foot plunge to the waiting dinghy, and if you were lucky, Henk would grab you before you bounced out. Invariably, in these conditions, everyone got wet either getting in or out of the Zodiac, or just from the spray while underway to the next boat.

Henk picked up our two Pauls and transferred them to *Chimera*, which would be leaving for Papeete immediately after the action. Paul Giles planned to stay on as crew of *Chimera* back to New Zealand. Young Paul would disembark in Papeete to meet up and spend a few days with Catherine before returning to New Zealand. We gave them both hugs goodbye and looked forward to reminiscing with them back in New Zealand. Henk then transferred two Daniels to us, one from *Chimera* and the other from *Tucker Thompson*. The *Tucker Thompson* had been on site for 16 days and was planning to leave for Rarotonga that evening. She did so in style, with all flags hoisted and a fireworks display from their vessel.

Both Daniels were from New Zealand and in their early twenties. Daniel Godoy had darker skin, and looked as though he may have been part Maori. He informed us that he was Chilean and had immigrated to New Zealand with his parents when he was very young. Daniel Salmon was involved in a film production class at the University of Auckland. He and his class partner, Martin Taylor, had come out on *Chimera* to make a video documentary of the Peace Flotilla efforts.

Because both Daniels had volunteered to go into the zone as part of a future action, it was not safe to put them on *Manutea*. The *Manutea* was of great strategic importance to the Peace Flotilla campaign; she was the only remaining Greenpeace vessel (besides the small sailboat *Vega*) and was equipped with satellite telephone and facsimile. The French military could confiscate the vessel if she was seen to be harbouring the 'zone runners'. We volunteered to take them as crew.

Dennis and I both enjoyed the new crew members. We spent a lot of time talking about our experiences, the Peace Flotilla efforts, Greenpeace, the French, what we should be doing as a group, and just hypothesising about what would happen next. We felt that we had a great deal in common with them. They were both committed to the peace effort and were planning their own action against the tests.

By nightfall, a 25–30-knot south-east wind blew up and we were blown 30 nautical miles from the general meeting location. The next morning we had to close the boat up tight and beat back to the line. It was a wet and miserable sail. This upset Dennis and he told me that he was sick and tired of bouncing from wall to wall.

"I'm bruised, bitchy, covered in salt and there is just this f*cking sea all around soaking us if we come on deck. There is no decent sleep and I loathe the perpetual smell of the boat; a sickly damp smell that I never want to smell again. It gets into everything, clothes, sleeping bag, and skin so that you seem to be part of the boat." "Relax, Dennis," I said. "Things will improve when the weather gets better."

We were unable to make it back to our assigned action location on time. We therefore went to the line a bit further south. We sailed a mile into the zone and surprisingly there was no French navy to greet us. We decided to pull back out of the zone, head north 10 miles then slowly drift back to our assigned action location by nightfall. We were becoming more experienced at using the wind and currents, which sometimes ran up to 3 knots, to help us minimise the sailing required to maintain position or get to where we wanted to go.

Just before nightfall, morale improved and we were singing and playing music. I looked up to see a patrol boat about 200 metres off our stern and coming down on us full steam, black smoke billowing from her stack. I yelled, "Hell! Action stations. The frogs are on to us." I shouted to Dennis to untie the propeller shaft stop. He scampered out of the companionway as fast as he could, jumped down in the engine-room and released it. I started the engine, grabbed the throttle and put *Joie* full ahead out to sea. We must have accidentally drifted into the zone again. I shouted down to one of the Daniels to check our position. Moments later he reported that we were outside the zone by 2 miles. We were OK.

"They scared the crap out of us, the bastards!" I said. It was obviously a ploy by the French captain to catch us off guard and surprise us. With their high powered surveillance equipment they could see that we were singing and enjoying ourselves and not paying attention to our location. As the patrol boat steamed by we could see the French sailors laughing on deck. They'd got even with us!

We went to the line that evening as planned, but behaved ourselves because the French patrol boat was nearby and kept a close eye on us.

In the morning we were looking forward to the return of the other boats to learn whether McTaggart was successful in getting someone into the atoll. With the high wind conditions, it was not a foregone conclusion. Later that afternoon we learnt that the *Chimera* crew, who sailed to the south-east side of the island to launch the action, were unsuccessful. The Zodiac had been holed so they abandoned the mission and sailed directly to Papeete.

The strong south-east winds persisted, creating uncomfortable living conditions and havoc for the flotilla. *Kela* reported that she had put out her parachute drogue to minimise drift. Nick noticed that one of the three braids holding the parachute had given way and they needed to get it in before the rest of the braids broke. To add to the problem, the painter of the dinghy they were towing got fouled in the ship's propeller, so Nick and Marty had to first dive under the boat in heavy rolling seas to untangle it. By this time the parachute broke loose from the boat and started drifting away. They were lucky to finally get it back on board. It was, however, quite a struggle and crew member Diarmuid ended up crushing his finger. They believed it was broken.

The course they indicated in that evening's sked with Nikao radio meant that they were under way to Papeete, obviously to seek medical attention. Additionally, Cath still was not well; they were tired, and it was time to go. They had been at sea for nearly a month.

We all knew it was tough constantly being tossed around in the middle of the ocean, but I had special admiration for both the Tuckers (*New Zealand Maid*) and Gales (*Kela*), who brought their young children along.

Nick, whose two children were 7 and 2 years old, told me on arrival at Moruroa that when he looked back on the passage he could see that many of their initial worries about having the kids on board were unfounded. He was surprised at their resilience and adaptability. Both of his kids thrived on the voyage. They did get bored at times and he and Cath often despaired at their lack of privacy and opportunity to rest unmolested by young demanding voices. He said the rest of the crew were very helpful and ensured they had an ample supply of books and games to vary the kids' routine.

Before our departure, a number of people who knew little of the sea and boats voiced their disapproval on 'talk back' radio and in the press about taking young children on such a dangerous mission. They considered the parents irresponsible. However, both the Tuckers and the Gales strongly believed in involving their children in everything they did. This built a strong family bond, and was how children learned about life.

With the departure of *Kela*, there were only five boats left in the flotilla: *Joie*, *New Zealand Maid*, *Photina*, *Vega* and *Manutea*. The flotilla was dwindling and the atmosphere at the last strategy meeting was sombre.

Although a number of other boats were still on their way to Moruroa, we heard that one had had to abandon her mission. News finally arrived about the fiasco the vessel *Kaunitoni* experienced. She had departed Fiji with 68 passengers on board, including several European politicians and the former Cook Islands Premier Sir Tom Davis. The ship's engine failed 350 nautical miles east of Rarotonga. A

Royal New Zealand Air Force Andover dropped repair equipment to the ship, but she could not be fixed at sea. The ship drifted for several days before the Cook Islands boat *Te Kukupa* reached her and took her under tow. The ship again struck trouble when she slammed into *Te Kukupa* in the middle of the night with great force after the patrol boat's engines overheated and shut down. Passengers initially thought the vessel was going to sink, but she eventually made it to Rarotonga where the mission was officially abandoned.

Location of some of the underground test sites, contaminated zones and faults caused by the tests. Map courtesy of: Greenpeace

It was time to write a song. I got out the guitar and harmonica and, with help from the Daniels and Dennis, composed *The Moruroa Blues*. This boosted our morale considerably.

The Moruroa Blues

Chorus:

       G7
We've got the Moruroa Blues
       G7
We've got the Moruroa Blues
       C
We're here to stop the bomb
                    G7
Because we all know it is wrong
       D
We've got to make a stand
                       G7
To pull the French heads out of the sand

       G7
It's been forty-one days
       G7
Since our feet have touched the ground
       C
We find it hard to sleep
             G7
Without being tossed around
       D
If we don't get out of this washing machine
                  G7
We will get agitated and turn real mean

       G7
All around Moruroa is a 12-mile exclusion zone
       C   G7
It is only our GPS that keeps our boat our own
            D
Because if we go inside
                G7
The French will have our hide

Chorus/Harmonica

       G7
They buzz us every day

With their frigates, 'copters and jet planes
C   G7
Lord, 4 weeks of this is enough to drive a man insane
          D   G7
But we wake up each morning to do it all over again

          G7
The French came and took the Greenpeace boats away
              C
There is only the Peace Flotilla left and now we are
          G7
here to stay
          D   G7
So it's now our job to lead the French astray

Chorus

          G7
We're out of carrots, onions and potatoes too
          C   G7
We're so hungry we'll even eat froggie stew
          D
But we would rather starve
                                          G7
Than give into Chirac's nuclear view

          G7
If we ever go to sea again, It will be too soon
          C
We want to spend the rest of our lives in our
          G7
living rooms
                  D
But you know what?
                  D
If they keep up this insane campaign
                                          G7
We'll come back and sing this song again

Harmonica

Monsieur, you would not want this again would you?

September 21
New Zealand Maid had left the previous day, leaving only four boats in the flotilla. Their fresh supplies were nearly all gone, they were low on water and they had a broken mizzen boom that needed repair. We heard from Daniel that there were strong tensions on board, which was par for the course. One of their children had a relapse of glandular fever and had turned yellow. Barbara was ready to go.

Before they left, they gave us some of their last provisions of onions and eggs. Jon was able to throw the onions across to us on a close pass, but the eggs would surely break in such a manoeuvre. He cleverly and very quickly designed a raft made from a 5-gallon jerry-jug cut in half. He put the eggs in it and floated it on the water for us to pick up. Dennis was desperate because he hadn't had any eggs during the whole trip. He was determined to succeed at all costs in retrieving the eggs, even if he had to jump in for them!

With gaff-hook in hand, Dennis stretched with all his body to reach the floating hoard. To his dismay, he missed them on the first two passes. On the third pass he finally succeeded and, with a mischievous grin on his face, he clutched the prize gently against his sternum, descended to the galley and immediately cooked some. He had reached Nirvana.

That night was sultry and dark and we could see the illuminating glow of Moruroa as we once again approached the line to launch an action. We were surprised to learn that there was a small town of sorts on Moruroa, and this was where all the light came from. It had a supermarket, shops, a pub, two cinemas, laboratories, an industrial site and plenty of accommodation. There were up to 1800 people living there, about 500 of them soldiers of the French Foreign Legion. The rest were scientists, technicians and bomb and service workers.

New Zealander Rachel Sanson and Belgian Roger Gregoor planned to take a Zodiac into Fangataufa Island that night. Rachel was off the German boat *Tara*, which had arrived the previous day from Fiji. Her enthusiasm was remarkable considering that *Tara* had experienced opposing winds the entire voyage. We heard later that they both managed to get into the lagoon and had a real good look around for 15 minutes before being detected and apprehended. The French authorities reported that they apprehended them just inside the Exclusion Zone, and they had not entered the lagoon. Greenpeace members reminded us that this island was still dangerously radioactive from a previous open air test series and one could not stay on it too long.

Upon their release from French custody, Rachel and Roger confirmed expectations that the next test was likely to be conducted at Fangataufa. They had reached the drilling rig in the middle of the lagoon and saw preparations under way, including the barge that was already in place to monitor the test. We expected it to be a large explosion of up to 150 kilotonnes. Greenpeace believed that the French used Fangataufa for the large explosions because Moruroa was too fragile after many underground tests there.

Now it was the two Daniels' turn to make a small-craft approach. We said our goodbyes and wished them luck. They were going in on a two-person surf ski. The flotilla was using whatever it had that floated to keep the campaign alive and active.

Photina, *Vega* and *Joie* all approached the line together at 3 a.m. so that no one boat could be accused of launching the craft and thus be apprehended. Two French frigates were cruising the line between us and the atoll and they obviously sensed something was up.

The plan was to launch the pink surf ski (named *Aotearoa Ark* by the Daniels) from *Vega* in the early hours of the morning so they could use the glow of Moruroa for navigation. By sunrise they would be two thirds of the way there and could use the compass to navigate the rest of the way. The surf ski was made of plastic, and therefore their chances of getting in before being detected by French radar were good.

Two days later we heard that they had made it all the way into the lagoon undetected, even though patrol boats at times were only a mile a way. It had taken them 5 hours to get there and they actually surfed the ski over the dangerous fringing coral reef into the lagoon. They spent some time paddling around the lagoon before deliberately attracting the attention of the French military. Daniel Salmon optimistically took with him the University of Auckland's video camera to record an interview with the base commander. He got no interview and had his camera confiscated. They were flown to Papeete and sent home.

Later we heard from Daniel that the French legionnaires were surprised to learn the pair were not professional protesters and did not belong to Greenpeace. They were just a couple of New Zealand blokes trying to give the French Government a message. They took with them 200 letters written by New Zealand school children to deliver to the Admiral. The legionnaires and gendarmes who held the pair were also surprised to hear there were non-Greenpeace people protesting on the flotilla boats including families with children.

We were glad their action turned out OK, but we missed their company. Now it was just Dennis remaining with me on *Joie*.

At a flotilla meeting on *Manutea*, we were offered a Mediterranean style lunch and a couple of cold beers to wash it down. What a luxury it was compared to the canned food concoctions we came up with on *Joie*!

After the meeting, McTaggart took Dennis and I forward to a private spot at the bow of the boat and we discussed the 'Tureian plan'.

One of the key men supporting this plan was Oscar Temaru, the Tahitian pro-independence leader. McTaggart said that Oscar's passport had been removed by the French authorities and he would no longer be able to participate in the action.

The plan called for *Manutea* to sail to Tureia, 70 miles north of Moruroa. There she would meet Oscar Temaru's sister and pick up 40 to 50 Tureians sympathetic to the cause. The Tureians were likely to help in the protest because their tiny island was heavily 'snowed' upon during the French Government's earlier open-air nuclear tests. Some say that the population's health suffered significantly.

The sort of treatment these fine people endured was evidenced in the testimonial of a French military helicopter pilot, Philippe Drynen. His testimony was reprinted in the book *Poisoned Reign* (Danielsson & Danielsson, 1977, 1986):

In June and July 1967, three tests were made at

Moruroa. The devices were small and therefore produced much less radioactivity than later A and H bombs. The first two had been detonated hanging down from a balloon but due to a technical mishap the third bomb exploded at sea level, which of course was more dangerous.

Two days later I flew to Tureia (126 kilometres north of Moruroa) to pick up two meteorologists who had been left there together with the population of about sixty persons at the time of the explosion. I was forbidden to wear the protective orange overall, so as not to alarm the population. But I put on my special boots and gloves. I spent three minutes on the atoll, just the time needed to take off the two meteorologists.

For my part I was given a special shampooing, after which I could join my mates; but the two meteorologists had to remain in the hospital on board. However, before being allowed leave in Papeete, I had to submit to a special examination which revealed the existence of radioactive iodine in my thyroid glands. The amount was slight but I had to remain under observation for 3 days. As for the meteorologists, they were kept for a week in the hospital at Hao. This was a thought-provoking experience.

Since I had had to be decontaminated after having spent only three minutes on Tureia and the meteorologists who had been there for a month needed more extensive treatment, how much more radioactivity must the islanders have absorbed? They had not been evacuated and had received no instructions as to how to protect themselves. They continue to eat the lagoon fish and coconuts, to handle palm leaves and stones. In other words they are living and procreating in a radioactive environment.

The entire population (around 50 people) was removed from the island in 1968 before another test series of open air thermonuclear explosions at Moruroa. They were hidden away as guests of the French CEP in an army camp at Mataiea, on the south coast of Tahiti. When the public began asking questions regarding their whereabouts, the French authorities explained that the people of Tureia just happened on their own accord to ask for a free trip to Tahiti only 2 days before the first nuclear blast. The authorities explained this sudden urge to make a trip as a desire to participate in the 14th of July celebrations. While in Tahiti, each family was given their own house with all modern conveniences, free meals in the first-class army restaurant, and daily bus trips to Papeete, some 50 miles away, to participate in the festivities.

We planned to put about 25 Tureians each on *Joie* and *Vega*, then sail together into Moruroa. Because Moruroa was believed to be an ancestral atoll used by the Tureians before the French occupation, they would go to claim their land back.

September 24

We heard the bad news that New Zealand's World Court case to stop the tests was dismissed. New Zealand tried to re-open its 1973–74 case against French atmospheric testing and asked the court to enjoin the test series until a full environmental assessment could be completed.

Re-opening the old case was the only way New Zealand could get the French Government back in court, because the French had withdrawn their recognition of the court's compulsory jurisdiction in 1974. The French Government accused New Zealand of deceiving them into attending the World Court hearing.

The judgement was dismissed partially because of the fact that the 1973–74 case addressed atmospheric testing only. The case had been closed in December 1974, when France gave its commitment to stop atmospheric testing. New Zealand had not bothered to re-open the case for 21 years, even though the French continued testing by going underground.

It was a shame that small countries like many in the South Pacific had no legal recourse against a large superpower country like France. France could simply apply the 'French way' technique to insulate itself against any objection; they just refused to recognise a court's jurisdiction. They argued that, as a sovereign country, it was nobody's business what it did.

A case against France could possibly have been successful if it had focused upon the environmental and health impacts of underground testing at Moruroa. The French authorities had mastered a political campaign in support of their testing: they had not allowed proper public scientific monitoring of the test effects; there had been only three limited independent scientific studies of Moruroa, none of Fangataufa and none regarding the stability of the island and possible radiation leakage; and very little information had been collected on the health of indigenous populations and bomb workers. There had also been a number of accidents at Moruroa, which would suggest that they had run a very haphazard operation.

Aboard *Joie*, Dennis cooked up some corn fritters for dinner. I baked more bread, this time wholemeal, oat, and soy yoghurt. I discovered the dehydrated soy yoghurt in a forward locker. The bread came out exceptionally well. By this point, everything more creative than a can of baked beans was really appreciated.

Upon the arrival of New Zealand boats *Sudden Laughter* and *Pickety Witch* the flotilla was once again buzzed at very low altitude by the French jet. We swam over to *Sudden Laughter* and met the crew: James, Christine, Nigel, John, Simon and Brian, who all looked to be in good spirits. They told us that they had received bad press when they returned to Gisborne to make repairs after the storm that had hit all of us shortly after departure from New Zealand. The lashings between the main cross-beams and the outer hulls began to stretch, requiring replacement. The customs officer had called their catamaran unseaworthy. They were required to undergo another Category One inspection before being allowed offshore again. They arrived safely at Moruroa and it was great to see some more reinforcements.

They delivered a bottle of rum for John Simpson on *Photina*. It was a gift from his Nelson friend. It was promptly opened and the cap was thrown away!

Pickety Witch had a short stay. After only a day or so, they were on their way back to Papeete. She was a small boat (28 feet long) with four people on board. It took them 30 days sailing to get to Moruroa, and they had had to stop in at Rarotonga for repairs.

We heard on the radio that *Guinevere*, another Auckland boat, had arrived, but we had not seen them yet. The supply boat *Machias*, a 60-foot schooner charted by Greenpeace, had also arrived from Papeete. They brought us some of the groceries we ordered by radio: very ripe pineapples, rotten celery, potatoes, coconuts, squash, soap and beer! 'Hinnano' was a bitter lager, very European tasting, and good, even warm!

Machias also brought six Tahitians, a couple of vakas and two inflatables with engines. This would be enough for the flotilla and Greenpeace to work with next week.

The *Anna* had arrived late the previous night, after a very long 43-day passage from Warkworth, New Zealand. The next morning we manoeuvred into position so that Martin could film the French military deliver their warning letters to them. The four crew aboard the French inflatable were not very happy that we were filming them.

The arrival of the new boats brought our numbers back up from four to eight: *Joie, Photina, Vega, Manutea, Machias, Guinevere, Anna* and *Sudden Laughter*. We felt like a formidable flotilla again!

Recently, the mood on board had become more irritable and seemed to change with the weather. On windy and wavy days, we could not wait to head home. On nice days with gentle seas, we became happy and content to stay longer. To help cheer us up, I cooked crepes suzettes for breakfast, just like mum used to make! Dennis cooked pancakes and fritters for lunch with our newly supplied spuds.

Later we heard a call on the radio of yet another vessel in the vicinity that planned to stop briefly at Moruroa. The crew was on a trip delivering the boat from Scotland to New Zealand. We overheard Brad Ives of *Manutea* asking how we would recognise them. The skipper, Jamieson, described his boat as being black with white topsides. We carefully looked around for a small boat and we were blown away when a huge ship as big as a mountain began rising from the horizon and coming our way. We cheered, "She's a bloody ocean-going ferry!" Indeed she was. She was a 265-foot ferry called *Suilven*. The ship was on her way to New Zealand to begin service on the Cook Strait run between Wellington and Picton.

The skipper was wonderful, offering his services and inviting us to hold our next campaign meeting on his vessel. The meeting had to be abandoned, however, when we found that it was virtually impossible to get on board. The walls of the ship were high and the sea was rough, making a boarding very dangerous. *Suilven* did manage, however, to off-load fresh bread, meat, beer and other goodies for the protest fleet.

Because of *Suilven*'s tight schedule, Jamieson had to press on to Wellington. On his way, however, he tested the French authorities by sailing into or very close to the Exclusion Zone. All the skippers were on *Manutea* listening to the radio conversation, and we broke out in hysterics. The French gave the ferry the customary strict warnings. Jamieson ignored the first warning and, after the second was given, he replied by saying something to the effect that "I don't know what you're talking about, mate. I'm just on my way to New Zealand and am doing nothing wrong, *Suilven* out." The *Suilven* sailed on, and the French allowed her to continue on her way. It would have been highly amusing to watch the commandos try to tackle this huge ship.

September 25

When *Manutea* sailed to pick up the Tureians, Martin Taylor, who initially transferred from *Chimera* to *Manutea*, joined our crew. Martin had become the de facto Peace Flotilla cameraman and was disappointed not to be going with *Manutea* to film the pick-up. He was asked to stay and film the next campaign action: Sanae Shilda, director of Greenpeace Japan, planned to enter the 12-mile zone. Sanae had a very strong following back in Japan. She transferred from *Manutea* to *Vega* in preparation for the action.

At 3 a.m. we sailed to a location near the line in order to send off our Japanese friend. She was very scared and had never done anything like this before. Sea conditions had to be very calm before the Greenpeace crew on *Vega* would risk letting her go. The plan was for her to go single-handedly into the Exclusion Zone and broadcast live on Japanese radio from the zone. This was our second attempt. The weather was too rough and the action was abandoned.

The flotilla set sail to the north part of the zone where we arranged to meet the *Manutea* returning with the Tureians on board for the next action. It blew 15 knots and we beat into a south-east wind under reduced sail, making 4–5 knots.

Later in the morning we heard our coded message over

the radio, 'No radio equipment required from *Joie*', meaning that we would not be needed to participate in the Tureian action. Greenpeace had only come up with 17 Tureians, instead of the 50 we had expected. Since all the passengers could fit on one boat, Greenpeace decided to use just *Vega* for the action.

This message took tremendous pressure off my shoulders. I was worried about what would happen to *Joie* once she was confiscated by the French authorities, and whether I would ever get her back. At the same time, I was disappointed that we would not be participating in one of the largest protest actions and the strongly symbolic gesture of taking the indigenous peoples back to their rightful islands.

McTaggart expected this action to be 'the big one', and one which might trigger more protest activity in Papeete. He would join *Vega* and go in with the Tureians. After the action, which we expected to result in the sacrifice of the veteran *Vega*, Greenpeace would need further assistance with other planned actions. We would probably stay for one or two more, then do a dash for home. We were getting very tired and, besides, it was becoming late in the season for returning to New Zealand.

The French military knew that something was going down when the flotilla arrived at the northern location of the 12-mile Exclusion Zone. A patrol boat steamed by at close range with crew on deck peering through binoculars. Charlie, the first mate of *Manutea*, came by to pick up Dennis and Martin for a meeting and confirmed that they had 17 Tureians on board.

The wind freshened, complicating the transfer of the Tureians from *Manutea* to the 38-foot *Vega*. A couple of Tahitians from the Tavini Independence Party were also joining the action, including Yvette Temaru, the half-sister of Tahitian independence leader Oscar Temaru. As veteran protesters Chris Robinson and David McTaggart would be joining them, there would be 21 people on board *Vega*.

It took four trips in the Zodiac to transfer the Tureians and other crew. We watched close by as old and young, large and skinny, male and female were pushed and hauled up onto *Vega*. No one was smiling. This was serious business, and it appeared that a number of them were seasick. They spread out around the small boat and soon the deck was strewn with bodies. A number had lain down flat on the deck to quell their seasickness.

With everyone on board, McTaggart gave a very powerful speech on VHF Channel 16 before heading for the line. He spoke calmly, and with great authority and confidence. His speech went something like this:

My name is David McTaggart, owner of the ketch *Vega*. I am speaking to you in peace on behalf of the 21 Polynesian people on board.

I realise you have strict instructions to stop any Peace Flotilla yacht from entering the 12-mile zone of Moruroa. Therefore, I request that you record the following message and forward it to your Admiral. We shall wait peacefully for a reply. We naturally expect a positive response, but if none is received within one hour, we will proceed anyway.

To the Admiral:

The people of Moruroa and many people of Polynesia have requested that I, David McTaggart on *Vega*, peacefully sail with representatives of the people into the lagoon at Moruroa atoll.

We are sailing due south straight to the passage into the lagoon. We realise that you respect the right of passage by a ship under sail. If your warships block our passage and cause any harm to the 21 men, women and children on board, we will hold you the Captain of the vessel, and President Chirac, personally responsible. We will sail peacefully into the lagoon with the intention of anchoring. The Polynesians on board wish to deliver a letter to the Admiral. We intend to stay overnight and for the people to sleep on the island, which is their own land, then get back on board *Vega* and sail straight out again.

There was no reply from the French and within 20 minutes *Vega* began motor-sailing towards Moruroa.

We, *Photina* and *Sudden Laughter* closely followed them to the line. McTaggart said on VHF radio, "Thank you New Zealand boats. Your support has been most welcome." I replied, "We will follow you to the line, but you get the line honours."

Even at a distance, you could see that McTaggart was in his element. He proudly perched himself on the stern of the boat steering the vessel onward with great determination. With bleach-white hair and wearing a white singlet, he stood out amongst the dark Polynesians who were scattered all around the deck.

The other flotilla boats including *Manutea* joined the escort. The flotilla was so aggressive that we unknowingly followed *Vega* over the line by about a mile as two distant French frigates steamed full ahead to the location.

Warning messages were sent by the French warship *La Nivose*. The French military sent four messages in all, asking *Vega* to change course. They were gentle at first, asking *Vega* to state their intentions, then finally ordering it to stand by for boarding and inspection.

Warning number 3 to *Vega*:

This is French warship *La Nivose*. It is 2 p.m. on the 26 of September. You are 2.5 miles into French territorial waters. If you do not change course to due north, you will come under French military discipline. Please stop your vessel for search and inspection.

Tui had just arrived on the scene, returning from Rarotonga. Just before McTaggart's speech, they radioed asking for an interview with the *Joie* crew. I said, "We are at a meeting now and cannot. Perhaps later."

We followed *Vega* as far as practicable and then changed course back out of the zone to due north, just as a French patrol boat came steaming up the rear.

At the same time *Tui* began broadcasting to all the flotilla boats that they were over the line and should proceed in a northerly direction towards them. *Tui* was standing out by about 5 nautical miles to the north.

'That's all we need now,' I thought to myself. 'Our own country's ship harassing us to get out of the zone, when we are participating in perhaps one of the most important actions of the protest campaign.' I replied to the *Tui* skipper, John Campbell, that according to our navigation we were not in the zone. I lied. I knew the French military would be listening.

We all watched as the two French frigates encroached upon the small *Vega*, which was virtually out of sight except for a glimpse of the mast. It looked like nothing more than a toothpick in the ocean between two mighty warships.

We heard shortly after that *Vega* had been boarded, seized and taken into Moruroa. Audrey Cardwell from *Manutea* broadcast over VHF radio what a disgrace it was. *Vega* gave a formal request to sail to Moruroa peacefully on behalf of 'the people who own this land', and their passage was blocked. Audrey kept us all informed as more information about the safety of the *Vega* crew and passengers came to light. She announced later that the French authorities would return the Tureians to their home island. McTaggart and Chris Robinson were held for at least 24 hours, then expelled from French Polynesia. They would never be allowed to return.

Soon thereafter, French authorities launched a propaganda campaign about the incident and accused Greenpeace of tricking and exploiting the Tureians. They claimed that the Tureians thought they were going on a fishing trip and had no idea where they were or what they were doing.

Audrey clearly refuted this claim in an SSB radio broadcast. She explained that it was actually insulting to the Tureians and ridiculous to suggest that people who lived in the area would not know where they were. The Tureians made the decision to go in full consideration of the possible consequences. They all had the chance to change their mind at the last moment. "The accusations were another example of typical French colonial attitudes," she said.

And of course she was correct. These were the people who lived no more than 70 miles from Moruroa. Moruroa was their back yard! What the French authorities didn't mention was the letter that the Polynesian people carried with them for delivery to the Admiral. The letter, translated into English, read as follows:

September 26, 1995

To the President of the Republic of France, Jacques Chirac and the Admiral of the French Navy.

We, the Maohi people, rightful owners of the atolls of Moruroa and Fangataufa, greet you. It has been 30 years that you have been conducting nuclear tests on these islands. We are here of our own free will to ask you, President Chirac and Admiral, to terminate all nuclear testing. We want to get back our lands which are in a state of nuclear pollution. We are going to ask the United Nations to help us clean up this pollution.

Please accept, Mr President and Admiral our sincere greetings, thank you.

With respect we ask to have an answer in 15 days. If we do not have confirmation within this time, we will take further action to settle this matter.

The Maohi People
Address: Tureia Fakamaru, Marihau Jean

September 27

Photina departed for Rarotonga after 24 days on station at Moruroa. It was a tremendous effort by John Simpson, Conn Flinn and Andy Baumgarten. We would miss them dearly. Of all the skippers, John Simpson made the biggest inroad with the French military. Shortly after *Photina*'s arrival at Moruroa John wrote the Admiral a letter requesting a meeting with him. John spoke very good French and whenever a warship passed close by John would radio and ask when he could expect a response to his letter. It made amusing listening and although neither Dennis nor I understood French, one could sense the gist of the conversation. John sounded very polite, proper and sincere in his request, while the Frenchman sounded apologetic and committed to providing a response.

Finally the day came. The French captain called John and said they had a letter for him to pick up from the Admiral. John told us that he was hoping the Admiral had invited him to dinner! Rather he wrote an apology for not being able to meet him because he was in Papeete. However, he invited John to visit him if he was ever in Papeete. John told us the Admiral wrote: 'It would be nice to meet you and talk as old sailors.' John also mentioned that he got the 'thumbs up' sign from a number of French sailors when he went to pick up the letter.

At the campaign meeting that evening we discussed the

importance of delivering Martin Taylor's film footage of the Tureian action to Papeete; the value of the event would diminish with time. The only film footage that the world media had available was from the French authorities.

Dennis and Martin proposed that Greenpeace charter a plane from Papeete to Tureia, the nearest airstrip, 70 miles north of Moruroa. One of the flotilla boats could sail up with the film and rendezvous with the plane. We volunteered to go if Greenpeace committed to charter the plane. This would cost them $US9,000. We understood that the Television New Zealand (TVNZ) crew on *Tui* were also trying to get some film back, so we called *Tui* and requested a meeting on *Joie*.

At dusk, Audrey and Henk came over to *Joie* in a Zodiac just as the TVNZ reporters were leaving. Audrey was yelling at the *Tui* tender as she was racing away with the journalists, 'We have a plane landing tomorrow morning at Tureia.' The tender would not stop. The helmsman was obviously under strict instructions not to meet with any Greenpeace representatives. If they did, the New Zealand Government could be construed as collaborating with Greenpeace.

Too bad for the TVNZ crew. They would not be able to get their film to market. We were leaving for Tureia immediately. Martin motored back with Henk and Audrey to *Manutea* to pick up the film and some more camera gear while Dennis and I changed sails. There was a light NE wind blowing so we hanked on our largest sail and shook the reefs out of the mainsail. When Martin came back we were off.

We had mixed feelings as we sped away. It was a great feeling to be going somewhere rather than heaving-to at Moruroa, but we also felt strange, as though we were leaving our home. We had no chart of Tureia but Henk, who had been there previously on *Manutea* to pick up the Tureians, gave me instructions. He told me that there was no pass into the atoll. Instead, there was a concrete wall and a small opening in the reef at the north end of the island for a tender to enter when the weather was favourable.

Tensions were high on *Joie* as we sailed north. Martin in particular was very restless. He had the job of going in with the film and getting on the plane when it landed. The situation was complicated by the fact that none of us on *Joie* had legally entered French Polynesia and Tureia was not a point of entry. So long as Dennis and I did not touch our feet on land we were legal, but Martin would be entering illegally and could be subject to the normal French discipline!

We heard that there was no French gendarme on the island when *Manutea* was there. But the islanders reported that a gendarme arrived before each test, so there was a high probability that one would be there. Martin's plan was to sneak ashore, hide by the runway, then run for the plane as it landed.

The three of us sat on deck and talked as we sailed through the night. "We'll be able to smell Tureia before we see it," I said. "Oh yeah? That's bull," said Dennis. "No, it's true," I said. "You can only see an atoll island from around 8–10 miles away, but you can smell them much further, especially if you are downwind, like we are. That's one of the techniques the early Polynesian sailors used to use to locate their island destinations. Another thing they look for were bright flashes of light deep down in the water; like someone taking a flash photo. If you see these, then you are close to land."

"You're joking," said Martin. "No, I'm not kidding", I said, "we are probably close enough to Tureia to see them now." With that, Dennis and Martin went to the bow of the boat and laid down on the deck with their heads hanging over the side, looking deep down into the clear Pacific ocean. "Wow", said Dennis. "There's one now." "Look," said Martin, "there's another flash. You're right Lynn. What causes them?" I explained that no one really knows what causes them. I suspected that they were some kind of phosphorescent plankton that pool together near islands and when boats sail over the top of them, they disturb them and they give off a flash. "That's cool", said Dennis.

We sailed throughout the night and just before dawn we could smell land. It was a nice spicy-sweet fragrance; an exotic smell, so pleasing to the palate that had tasted only salt air for the last 5 weeks. We saw a thin line of darkness just ahead as the dawn began growing into sunrise. There it was, the island of Tureia. It smelled beautiful and had sandy beaches covered with a thick growth of coconut palms. It was longer than we had expected and we had to make a decision whether to go up the east or west side to reach the north end. We turned right and went up the eastern side. In hindsight this was the wrong choice as it took twice as long to get to the village.

We arrived just offshore from the village an hour before the plane was due to land and launched our 8-foot fibreglass dinghy. Dennis and Martin piled into it with the film and Martin's belongings. He was not returning.

Dennis planned to run the pass between the breaking coral reefs, drop Martin off with the goods, then row back with the dinghy. I would stay on *Joie* to maintain our position offshore and assist if necessary.

The winds were untypical, blowing from the north at 15 knots, and there was a large swell breaking on the pass exposing sharp protruding coral heads all around. 'This could hardly be called a pass,' I thought. Rather, it was the best place to approach the island, and not a very safe one at that, especially when the wind was blowing from the north.

I watched Martin row as Dennis sat in the back. I could see fear on their faces as they approached the mass of breaking water. They could not even tell where the true channel was in the foaming sea. They decided not to make the attempt at the pass, and rowed back to *Joie*. Martin threw up his bag and asked me to grab the film and put it in plastic bags. I was amazed that he had not already done this, when the film was so precious.

Dennis complained bitterly that this was a dangerous and stupid act. His face was stern and very serious. He suggested that Martin should go by himself to keep the weight down in the dinghy, and to leave the dinghy behind. I was not in favour of giving up the dinghy, so they tried again. This time the film was protected in plastic bags. Again, they manoeuvred in front of the pass, waiting for a quiet spell in the waves, which did not occur. They chickened out and came back. Dennis was adamant. "I am not doing this f*cking thing for the sake of a dinghy, it is too dangerous!"

Both Martin and Dennis came back on board. Dennis said, "We were crapping bricks out there! No way we can get across that without taking the plunge; and that would be real nasty." Before Dennis could continue with his speech, I said, "I accept your decision. It is too dangerous. I am surprised it took you this long to come back!"

The locals, who were watching our plight from the

beach, launched their motor boat. Their launching technique was interesting. A bulldozer carrying the boat in its raised scoop came down to the concrete wall and lowered her into the water. The driver of the boat started the outboard motor, waited for a calm spell, then throttled the engine in full, planing the boat quickly over the reef and into the outer part before the next swell crashed over the pass. It was a tricky and dangerous exercise even for the local Tureian in a 18-foot motor boat. Dennis and Martin wouldn't have had a chance.

The motor boat came out to us and we explained to the driver, a Tureian man, as well as we could that Martin was going to Papeete. He only spoke French and Tahitian but, through a bit of sign language, we managed to communicate. He took Martin on board and went back to the island, again waiting 3–4 minutes at the pass entrance to get his timing right, before gunning the engine and slipping in over the reef.

If Martin was successful in getting out on the plane, he would ask the pilot to fly by us and flap the plane's wings. We would wait for this signal before leaving.

We saw the plane land and a half an hour later Martin called us from the plane's radio. He said that there was no gendarme on the island and that all was fine. A Greenpeace employee had come out from Papeete on the plane to make sure all went well. His name was Manuel. He came on the radio and thanked us for all our help. They took off, and the plane buzzed us twice before leaving, flapping its wings on both passes. Dennis and I both laughed because we knew from our time with Martin exactly what he was telling the pilot: 'Can you fly a little closer to *Joie* so I can get some shots from the air? Can you make one more pass at a lower altitude so I can get a better shot? Be sure to flap your wings.'

After a lunch of fried potatoes, Dennis and I set sail back to Moruroa. Mission accomplished. We felt relieved and satisfied. Later we learnt that the film footage was picked up by top news agencies such as Reuters and broadcast world-wide on BBC news. It completely contradicted the French official statement that the Tureians were manipulated by Greenpeace and they did not know where they were or what they were doing. That made our efforts seem worthwhile. The real story about the Tureian action got out!

Shortly after our return to Moruroa we had a surprise visit from Hugo Mansfield from *Tui*. He had come to interview us about our trip as part of a Peace Flotilla project for the Turnbull Library. We had a wonderful talk which he recorded on tape. We then played our *Moruroa Blues* song for him. He really liked it and asked permission to play it over the intercom for all the *Tui* crew to hear.

Later that day we heard from *Manutea* that four people had gone into Fangataufa in a Zodiac: Cathy Baker (New Zealand); our good friend Henk Haazen (Netherlands); the Director of Greenpeace Japan, Sanae Shida; and an Australian who came out on *Machias*, Damian Meagher.

Cathy and Damian had been dropped off at the entrance to the lagoon and managed to wander around the atoll for some time before being picked up by commandos who flew from Moruroa in a helicopter. Henk and Sanae were involved in a high-speed inflatable chase inside the lagoon near a drilling platform. A larger French inflatable eventually drove up over the edge of the Greenpeace inflatable badly fracturing Sanae's knee. She was bleeding and had to see a doctor. The French authorities flew Greenpeace activists Henk and Sanae to Paris, then deported them from France. Cathy and Damian were released in Papeete.

These little actions were very difficult and dangerous to perform. The inflatable crew had to leave at night, under cover of darkness, and navigate through an open ocean, sometimes with large sea swells, to find the lagoon's tiny entrance. A number of dangers confronted them: should the engine fail they would drift hopelessly at sea; they could be capsized by a large wave; they could hit the reef and be thrown onto the razor sharp coral; or they could be run down by a French frigate.

These actions, as frivolous as they may have seemed, were a constant source of embarrassment to the French Government. We heard through the grapevine that the base commander came under severe criticism from his superiors for not being able to stop the protest flotilla from breaching the zone, landing and, in some instances, spending considerable time on the atolls. They understood the significance of these small actions in attracting negative media attention for the testing programme.

In launching this latest action, the crew of *Anna* told us that they acted as a decoy for *Manutea* when they both travelled south down the east side of the two islands. *Anna* stopped occasionally and put on their spreader lights, which lit up the whole deck, and acted as if they were busily doing things topsides. When this drew the warship to their location, *Manutea* launched the inflatable from their location in the dark.

On their return to the general meeting location, the crew of *Anna* told us that they had drifted over the line by 2.5 miles and were told by the French military to heave-to and prepare for search and seizure. French commandos came on board and interrogated the crew, looking for propaganda pamphlets that they claimed would be used to stir up trouble in Papeete. Once the *Anna* crew told them they would be returning to New Zealand by way of Rarotonga, the French let them go with a verbal warning not to enter the zone again. This was the first vessel which had been boarded by French commandos in the zone and not seized!

After this incident, the French military seemed to know what was going on within the Peace Flotilla. It was suggested by Greenpeace that the French may have used the opportunity to place a bug on *Anna*. It seemed out of character that they would board the vessel, search it, but not seize it.

Dennis attended another campaign meeting aboard *Manutea* and came back with instructions for our next action. Three Tahitians who came out on the supply boat *Machias* with their outrigger canoe would paddle to Moruroa, providing the weather was suitable.

Three code phrases had been devised and one would be announced over the radio. (1) '*Anna*, your rudder is fixed', meant the outrigger canoe would go that night and all flotilla boats should move to the same location on the line. (2) '*Anna*, your rudder is not fixed', signalled that the action had been called off. (3) '*Sudden Laughter*, we appreciate your Radio Liberty Show', meant that it was too rough for the outrigger canoe, but we would instead conduct a general action to keep the French busy. This involved going to the line at midnight in several different locations.

The Radio Liberty Show signal was broadcast by *Manutea*. By now, Dennis and I were getting tired of getting up or staying up to 'toe the line'. But we did it and got our customary warning from the French frigate. I guess we went in a little too far again!

After the action, we determined that we were out of the zone and changed course, heaving-to in a direction that would gradually take us further away from the zone. It was 1 a.m., rainy with squalls and significant wind shifts. We were tired, so we both went to our bunks.

We were startled from deep sleep by a loud voice and a very bright light. 'Now you don't often get that at sea,' I thought. A Frenchman was yelling on a megaphone, "You are in French territorial waters." Dennis jumped from the main cabin in the nick and yelled, "The frogs are here. Get up!" It was pitch black outside except for a 4000-candle-power beam totally lighting up our vessel and blinding us. I could make out the shape of a huge warship towering above us. It was only 25 metres away.

They must have realised that we were sleeping, as we scrambled to the deck putting on our clothes at the same time. Dennis, in a frenzy, jumped down into the engine room and untied the propeller shaft and I started the engine. I motioned to the French ship that we were on a course out of the zone, turning my head to the side to avoid looking directly into their blinding spot light. They seemed to be satisfied and sailed away. Dennis and I had a chuckle – they got us again, the bastards!

CHAPTER 9

Onward to Papeete

By September 30, we had been at Moruroa for 21 days and at sea for 40. Dennis and I were getting a bit tired and looked forward to some terra firma. We felt that we had done our dash and that it was time for some of the more recent arrivals (*Anna, Sudden Laughter, Te Kaitoa* and *Guinevere*) to continue with the campaign.

That evening we said goodbye to all the crew of *Manutea* whom we had got to know so well. Alex, the radio operator with a gorgeous Zimbabwe accent; Brad Ives, the coolest and calmest skipper that one could ever imagine; Charlie, the first mate and also calm but not quite as cool!; April, the friendly and attractive cook, whose meals we shared on a number of occasions; and Audrey Cardwell, the campaign co-ordinator who functioned like a corporate executive, but who had a very strong affection for the anti-nuclear movement.

Hugs and kisses went all around and Michelle Seather, a Greenpeace activist from Australia, gave us a lift back to our boat. We said goodbye to her then.

We weren't just going to set sail and leave though. That would be too easy! Fifteen of the Tureians who had participated in the *Vega* land claim-back action were stuck in Tureia after the French authorities had returned them there. They needed transport to the neighbouring island of Vanavana where *Manutea* had originally picked them up. They had been living and harvesting copra on the island. Vanavana was 31 miles to the west of Tureia.

Brad Ives, who had initially picked them up in *Manutea*, had agreed to return them to Vanavana. Greenpeace was, however, expecting the 'big one' to go off any day and Audrey would not allow *Manutea* to leave the site of Moruroa. So

'Intense' Tureian protesters! Joie had to transport the 15 Tureians who participated in the land-claim action at Moruroa back to the island of Vanavana where they were harvesting copra. They were excellent musicians and singers and we had great fun together.

Goodbye to all our new friends. They were friendly, simple and fun-loving people and we were sad to say goodbye.

Above Left: French commandos approach MV Greenpeace *in international waters. They confiscated and disabled it, then towed it to the distant atoll of Hao. Photo by Greenpeace.*

The Rainbow Warior *in the process of being seized by the French inside the Exclusion Zone at Moruroa. Photo by Greenpeace.*

Above & opposite page top right: French commandos storm Rainbow Warrior *tear-gas the bridge and disable her. Photo by Greenpeace.*

Greenpeace crew members from Rainbow Warrior *and MV Greenpeace were taken into custody, handcuffed, then transported by plane from Moruroa to Papeete. No-one was ever charged. Photo by Greenpeace.*

The last Greenpeace vessel to be confiscated by the French: the Caramba. *She joined us and the other New Zealand boats,* Sudden Laughter *and* Te Kaitoa, *in an anti-nuclear protest in Papeete Harbour.*

We protested in front of the frigate La Nivose *which was moored at the navy base in the west end of Papeete Harbour. This frigate had seized the* Vega *and*

The French could not resist getting involved. Here the Caramba is being arrested by the harbour Police for 'illegally moving in the harbour'. All protest boats received a citation, were escorted to anchorage, then held under 'boat arrest'. We were told we could not leave Papeete until our case went to court the following week. The potential penalty was 10 days in jail and a $US10,000 fine.

Manutea and harassed the Flotilla while at Moruroa. Upon approaching the vessel, we were greeted by two inflatables full of French military in combat gear. On the shore riot police assembled.

Saying our good-byes before leaving for the 5-6 day sail from Papeete back to Moruroa to close out the Peace Flotilla campaign. From left to right: Bonnie, Manutea cook; Tahitian friend; John Frost; Ingrid Gordon; Charlie, first mate

Manutea; *John Mate, Caramba campaign co-ordinator; Lynn Pistoll; Jacqui;*
Manuel & Glyn Walters, Greenpeace Papeete.

After the third explosion we all felt sad and remorseful. It was impossible to stop the French from their nuclear madness. We all gave speeches over the VHF radio as part of our campaign closing ceremony. The last two protest boats, Joie *and* Caramba, *then sailed for home. From left to right: Dennis Johnson, John Frost and Ingrid Gordon.*

"But what the hell, we're now going home!"

Dennis and I volunteered to pick up the Tureians at Tureia, transport them to Vanavana, then carry on to Papeete. It sounded like a nice way to go out, and I really wanted an opportunity to spend several hours with some Polynesian people who, from past experience, I had always found to be friendly and warm. And these Tureians just weren't ordinary Polynesians, they were heroes for bravely going into Moruroa.

So Dennis and I set sail that evening. We were still tired from the previous night's ordeal with the French, and were not looking forward to the long night sail. I opened a bottle of wine and we toasted our departure from Moruroa. Sad feelings ran through both of our hearts as we left the little 'city' behind. We could see the lights of all the flotilla boats fade slowly as we headed north. Yes, this did seem like home and we were leaving it. On the bright side, we looked forward to meeting our Polynesian passengers and then going on to Papeete, some 620 nautical miles to the west.

A 12-knot southerly wind pushed us north in light seas. It was a comfortable sail (for a change) and we made good time, arriving at Tureia at dawn.

October 1

Manutea had a 6 a.m. sked with the Tureians, who also had an SSB radio on the island. The Tureians did not know that we were coming in *Manutea*'s place to transport them to Vanavana. Brad Ives would talk to the Tureians from Moruroa in French and explain that *Joie* was *Manutea*'s replacement. He would further explain what they were to do: bring something to eat for the passage and leave the pigs and chickens behind!

I could not raise *Manutea* on the radio, and neither could Tureia. I suspected that something was amiss. My suspicion was later confirmed. *Manutea*, the last remaining Greenpeace boat, had been seized by the French military and taken into Moruroa.

So I did the best I could to communicate to the Tureians over the radio, "*Joie* Tureia a Vanavana, *Joie* Tureia a Vanavana. No *Manutea*, no *Manutea*." I repeated this over and over again. I do not speak any French and had no French dictionary on board. They somehow got the message!

Although the pass was again very rough, two Tureians

managed to launch a motor boat and came out to explain in sign language that they were all in church. It was a Sunday. They would meet us at 11 a.m. with the passengers at the north-east end of the island after Mass. It was too rough to use the pass, so they would launch a boat from the north-east point of the island, where there was the least swell and wind. It was 7 a.m. and we had 4 hours to wait. The Polynesians are very religious and Mass came first, even before being transported back to their own village.

At 10.30 a.m. we motored around to the north-east end of the island and were met by a large open decked red boat full of Tureians. It was a very colourful sight. They were all wearing bright and cheerful clothes that accentuated their dark tanned skin. They came alongside and a flurry of activity hit us. Dennis and I could hardly believe it as people clambered on and began briskly unloading supplies. Enough supplies and belongings came on board to fill half of the main cabin. We had everything from mattresses to plants (tapioca root). They unloaded their boat in the space of 2 minutes and the tender broke away, with the driver waving goodbye to all his friends.

With 15 Tureians sprawled all over the deck, we managed to get the sails up and were under way for our estimated 5-hour sail. Now the fun began, as we could not speak their language and they could not speak ours. But through sign language we were able to communicate and have a lot of laughs. Actually Dennis and I concluded that they were laughing at us! We both looked rather scruffy by this stage.

I broke out the guitar and mandolin and soon we had lots of wonderful Polynesian music. Quite a number of the Tureians could play the instruments and sing well. The instruments were passed around, and with each new player we had a different tune. This was obviously the Polynesian solution to not having CD players! I played the mandolin with one of them playing the guitar, and another singing, and we made some very nice music together. Polynesian music is very expressive and beautiful. I wish I could have understood the lyrics. No doubt they were moving words.

A number of the men were handsomely tattooed and

had Rastafarian style hair. I asked one guy his name and he joked, 'Bob.' I asked, 'Bob Dylan?' He said, 'No, Bob Marley!' and the whole group of Tureians broke out in laughter.

Dennis and I noticed how free and easy going they were, including their sexual expressions. For example, 'Bob Marley' sat in one corner of the cockpit talking to a young Tureian girl who was sitting opposite him. As he was speaking to her he would rub his groin until his member firmed under his pants. He then took his hand away and showed the bulge to the girl. The other men sitting close noticed the activity and joined in with laughter. The girl would play along and return a verbal gesture in retaliation.

After a 5½ hour sail, we arrived at the beautiful atoll of Vanavana. It was a small atoll, about 6 miles in diameter, but what a tropical paradise! Unfortunately, there was no pass; Dennis and I would have loved to have stayed a day or two.

When we left Wellington, Marianne had given Dennis a small plant. He had been faithfully looking after it for the whole trip and planned to plant it at Moruroa as a source of life and hope. Because he never made it to Moruroa, he knew Marianne would approve of his giving the plant to the Tureians, the ancestral owners of Moruroa, to plant on Vanavana.

We said our goodbyes and hugged several of the men. We gave them a box of food containing biscuits, butter and muesli bars. Dennis presented the plant to them. He didn't know what it was, so told them it was camellia. They were delighted with it and said they would plant it on the island. Soon a tender arrived and the Tureians piled into it with their gear. It took three trips this time, as the boat was smaller than the one on Tureia.

Dennis and I both felt sad to see them go and we were amazed at how we had developed such a bonding relationship with these people in such a short time. Moisture crept into our eyes as we set sail for Papeete, 620 nautical miles to the west.

As I adjusted the Aries self-steering vane, I noticed that the Tureians had forgotten their empty 60-gallon drum that was tied to the back of the boat. We dropped the sail, motor sailed back close to the shore and waved for attention. As it was very difficult to come out through the surf again they waved us to keep it and go on.

Of course this was the last thing I needed on the boat; a huge drum tied to the pushpit. So Dennis got a plastic bag and some tape and sealed the holes in the top of the drum. We motored up wind and close to the shore and heaved it in, thinking that it would be blown on shore and retrieved later by the Tureians. Despite our precise calculations, the drum appeared to float along the shoreline on a course that would eventually miss the island. We continued sailing to Papeete anyway justifying that it would eventually find a useful home on one of the islands. It was made of plastic so was not a danger to vessels. As we sailed away, we were relieved to see an outrigger canoe being launched from the island to rescue it.

Brad had warned us that the Tureians were likely to nick a few things. He explained that they had a 'communal property' attitude about possessions. Dennis and I did a quick inventory and discovered that some of our toiletries (Bic razors) had been nicked. Also gone was my Casio watch, which had evidently been greatly admired. It had been strapped to the rack above the chart table. This left a bit of a sour taste, especially since I relied on the watch for navigation. Dennis and I tried to understand how these people could spend the whole morning in church, then steal from those who were helping transport them back to their home village. In the end we gave up pondering it and just accepted this aspect of their culture.

BOOM! French Explosion Number Two

It was Sunday afternoon, 1 October 1995, and we heard on the radio from *Sudden Laughter* that the French exploded their second bomb at Fangataufa Atoll. *Tui*, which was still on site, confirmed it. It was a big one, about 110 kilotonnes, roughly equivalent to an earthquake 5.9 on the Richter scale and about eight times the size of the bomb dropped on Hiroshima. We later heard speculation through the grapevine that this test had served to validate the TN75 warhead which would equip France's new generation of nuclear submarines from the middle of 1996.

Sudden Laughter also reported that *Manutea* had been

grabbed the previous night after the outrigger canoe was finally launched with the three Tahitians in it. It all made sense: remove the Greenpeace boat then blow the bomb. This way there was no interference and no negative campaign material leaving the atoll.

The French bomb administrators obviously had planned the explosion for a Sunday morning, knowing that most Polynesians would be in church. Tactically, this would minimise the chance of another full-scale riot in Papeete. Polynesians are faithfully religious people and Sunday is a sacred day to them. This act would be seen as an insult to their religion. That Sunday the French Government demonstrated a new depth in their arrogance, not only with respect to the local Polynesians, but also to the Christian faith world-wide, especially their own Christian heritage.

Their 'damage control' tactics also included shutting off all news media access to Moruroa; no press trips to the site would be allowed. An additional 700 riot police were also flown into Papeete even though leading pro-independence activists who had participated in the last riot were still being held in jail.

We encouraged *Sudden Laughter*, who were still on site, to continue with the campaign updates which *Manutea* had broadcast. *Sudden Laughter* had Inmarsat and a fax on board and had become the primary campaign vessel.

Needless to say, the French tactics worked well and we heard of no ensuing rioting in Papeete.

The rest of the world bitterly complained again, but it fell on deaf ears. The South Pacific Forum finally got tough and suspended France from post-forum dialogue. Another wave of protests were launched against French embassies world-wide, including a protest of more than 10 000 people in Berne, Switzerland. How France could continue to test these weapons against the opinion of almost the entire world and the majority of her own population was almost beyond comprehension.

It was a 4-day sail to Papeete from Vanavana before 25-knot south-east winds. The sea was sloppy but we managed to run goosewinged the best part of the way.

We arrived at 5 p.m. on the 5th of October. We were too

late to clear customs, so we were quarantined until 9 a.m. the following morning. We sat on the boat all night marvelling at the bustling town of Papeete from our boat. Being so close to land, the temptation to go ashore was almost irresistible. After some 40 days at sea we could not leave the boat; it was like being in jail.

Joie was anchored peacefully and motionless in the harbour. It was the first time *Joie* had been absolutely still since August 23 when we left Wellington. We couldn't believe how wonderful it felt. There was no rocking, no watches, and we looked forward to sleeping the full night without a worry.

We were surprised to see Greenpeace's Michelle Seather and April (the cook), who had been on *Manutea* when she was seized, come out to greet us as we moored up. Later Dave, from *Machias*, which was moored next to us, came over on his way to the grocery store and asked if we needed anything. We gave him money to buy beer and chocolate bars. We enjoyed them as we sat on *Joie* watching and listening to all the night activity on the Papeete waterfront.

Because of our quarantine we missed a very large demonstration that night organised by pro-independence leader Oscar Temaru. Thousands of Polynesians participated in the peaceful march, carrying torches and singing. The Greenpeace people said it was one of the most moving experiences they had ever had. These people had been fighting for independence from France and the bomb for over 50 years. They believed that the French Government were denying them the right to independence in order to continue using the Polynesian Islands as a nuclear test bed.

Daniel Mares from *Caramba*, the Greenpeace-owned sailing yacht moored next to us, rowed over and told us that France had announced that it would sign the Nuclear-free Pacific Treaty with the US and UK in 1996. France also promised to continue to pay an amount of money over the next 10 years to help support the Polynesian economy. This was great news and obviously our presence and the pressure from the rest of the world had turned France's hand. But this was still not good enough – they should abandon the on-going test programme now.

The next morning Dennis and I went ashore and we

both knelt down and kissed the ground. Then Dennis got up and started running away. I shouted, "Where are you going?" He yelled, "I just want to get more than 20 feet away from you for a change!" I had a good laugh and let him go on. I thought how remarkable it was that we both had managed to live all that time in a space smaller than most people's bathrooms; one that was being tossed around continuously. It was beyond me how we had managed not to tear each other apart; we had a good working relationship.

On the way to Customs we saw a number of shops and restaurants that had been burnt out and gutted during the riot. 'Wow,' I thought. 'This was some major uprising'. We cleared Immigration and Customs and were given 5 days to stay without posting a bond of US$750. We walked up to the market and got some fresh fruit, vegies and bread, then walked to the Greenpeace office to meet the staff and the rest of the *Manutea* crew, most of whom were still in town.

We learned from them that on the day *Manutea* was seized, she was boarded in international waters at 5 a.m. by a large group of French commandos. They claimed the right to seize the vessel according to the law of 'hot pursuit'. They said that because the infringing outrigger canoe had been launched from *Manutea*, she was guilty. The *MV Greenpeace* had been seized under the same law when her helicopter had breached the Exclusion Zone then returned to the ship in international waters.

Michelle Seather had just managed to get a 20-second phone call to the Greenpeace office in Papeete before their communications were cut. They were taken into Moruroa, told to take only one bag, and were immediately put on a plane and transported to Papeete. While they were in the air the second bomb was detonated. In Papeete they were fingerprinted and photographed but not charged! They were released in Papeete. However, Brad Ives, the skipper, was detained, questioned, then expelled to New Zealand where we learned he was welcomed by the media and conducted a news conference.

All of the other flotilla vessels – *Guinevere*, *Sudden Laughter* and *Anna* – had left Moruroa and were on their way to Papeete or Rarotonga. *Anna* was the last to leave.

Greenpeace, who were concerned about the lack of a presence at Moruroa, hired *New Zealand Maid* to take Audrey Cardwell back out to location. Dennis and I were surprised to hear that they were going back for another go. Jon and Barbara, however, had always been staunch protesters against nuclear proliferation. They came to do a job and this would surely cap it off for them.

Barbara and the two younger sons of the Tucker family decided to stay in Tahiti, while Jon and his crew made the long and arduous trek back against the prevailing trade winds. *New Zealand Maid* was not an ideal windward boat. Her shoal draft and old-fashioned rig were great downwind, but not designed for tacking efficiently. They had to motor-sail all the way back to Moruroa. This took 6 days and consumed most of their fuel supply.

We had a number of meetings with Greenpeace representatives in Papeete and Dennis and I noticed a lot of confusion with the current policy on the testing. There appeared to be a lack of commitment, equipment and financial resources to continue a strong and active campaign. That was understandable: the French military had confiscated all Greenpeace protest vessels and equipment (except the 47-foot sloop *Caramba*). And what a collection it was! They had the 38-foot ketch *Vega*, the 170-foot ex-North Sea side trawler *Rainbow Warrior*, the 180-foot ex-ocean going tug *MV Greenpeace*, the 112-foot chartered schooner *Manutea*, and *La Ribaude*. They had also confiscated 23 inflatable craft, tonnes of supplies, navigation equipment and a helicopter.

Further confusing the situation was a changing of the guard at the Papeete Greenpeace office. Lynnette Thorstensen, the person in charge and the one who had run the campaign from the beginning, was going back to Australia. She was replaced by Janet Dalziell from New Zealand. Janet was only in place for a short while before she was replaced by Glyn Walters from Auckland. He would be there for only a week! Meanwhile, John Mate arrived from Canada, and he would be replacing Audrey Cardwell as the campaign co-ordinator. He would travel on *Caramba* to Moruroa.

We proposed to Greenpeace that we would consider continuing with the campaign if there was something worth doing. We were torn between the financial and emotional demands to return home and the anti-nuclear cause. Dennis and I talked it over and decided we were satisfied with the contribution we had made to the campaign and we were content to return to New Zealand. Furthermore, the hurricane season would begin on the first of November.

Dennis and I asked for a meeting with Greenpeace. We were pleased Janet Dalziell and Michelle Seather requested that we hold the meeting on the beach under a coconut palm tree, in such a lovely setting. However, Janet explained that the real purpose for the location was that the Greenpeace office and telephones were bugged by French Intelligence. She told us of a recent incident where one of the staff picked up the phone to make a call and heard her voice from an earlier conversation being played back to her!

It was obvious from our meeting that Greenpeace did not have an explicit campaign policy and they asked us for ideas. Dennis revealed one of the plans we had concocted while sailing to Papeete. It continued on the theme of 'surrounding Chirac', by executing a protest at Hao Island; another link in the chain. In the past the French had assembled bombs at Hao and had still used it in association with the bombing programme at Moruroa. Also, *Rainbow Warrior* and *MV Greenpeace*, confiscated earlier in the campaign, were still held there.

The French authorities would not be prepared for an 'attack' on Hao and it would be easy for a sailboat to sail into the lagoon, off-load several Zodiacs with crew, and take over the island (symbolically speaking, anyway). Greenpeace liked the idea and put forward a proposal to Greenpeace headquarters in Washington DC. They would let us know in a day or two whether the plan would be approved.

In the meantime we worked on our list of boat repairs while waiting for an answer. Nothing arrived and Michelle Seather, who had supported our Hao proposal, left for Europe. Given that Greenpeace did not have a clear plan or sufficient financial commitment to continue a concerted campaign, Dennis and I decided that we would head home. We did not tell Greenpeace officially but word got out and everybody knew of our decision. Dennis and I were relieved that a decision had been made.

Greenpeace decided to finish the campaign by sending their last boat, *Caramba*, to Moruroa to bear witness to the testing. Daniel Mares, an ex-skipper of *Vega* and past crew member of *Rainbow Warrior*, came from New Zealand to help prepare and equip *Caramba*. *Caramba* was a 47-foot sloop that initially joined the Peace Flotilla from Auckland. Apparently there were many difficulties with the boat and crew, and she returned to Papeete after only a limited stay on location at Moruroa.

Daniel was a very easy going, modest and likeable person. He had a huge task ahead of him. Practically everything imaginable had to be repaired on *Caramba*; the engine, navigation equipment, radios, sailing gear, toilet, etc. The previous crew had simply abandoned it, as it was, after arriving at Papeete. Even rotting stores were found in the hold. However, Daniel calmly defined and attacked the problems in a regimented fashion, leveraging additional resources and finance where he could to achieve his objectives.

On the day before our planned departure for New Zealand, I rowed over to *Caramba*, where Daniel and crew were frantically working to get the Greenpeace vessel up to scratch. Daniel invited me aboard and we had a long talk. In his very diplomatic manner, he proposed that the two boats *Joie* and *Caramba* sail to Moruroa to finish and properly close off the campaign. Two boats would be much better than one for safety reasons, for protection against the French military and for company. There would be no actions against the French this time. The boats and crew would be there to bear witness only. *Caramba* would be equipped with the latest Inmarsat communications and we would be able to speak to the rest of the world.

I liked the plan. It was clean and tidy. Dennis was just returning to *Joie* from a trip ashore, so I yelled at him to row over for a little chat. He had a feeling something was up. Although Dennis's mind was more set on going back to New Zealand, knowing him well I was sure he would change tack. As we talked, his eyes lit up like a Christmas tree and he accepted the plan as easily as a child would accept a sweet. We were both really attracted to the plan's objective of bearing witness. The plan provided a clear goal and the means to achieve it.

As we spoke, we agreed that *Joie* could accompany *Caramba* as long as the mission was seen as a joint exercise between the Peace Flotilla and Greenpeace. This meant that we would have access to the Inmarsat communications equipment on board *Caramba*. We were excited with the prospect of talking with the press in New Zealand and giving live interviews on site from Moruroa over the telephone. This was one thing that was sorely missed with the flotilla's first and main onslaught on the atoll.

We also needed Greenpeace to assist in the provisioning costs for *Joie*. We were already deeply in debt (in more than one way) for this cause.

Daniel, with his Greenpeace hat on, felt 99 percent sure that our requests would pose no problem.

A new feeling of elation enveloped Dennis and me, and Daniel too, no doubt. It was a good plan. We presented it later that evening to Janet Dalziell, and Manuel, who agreed in principle. It was all go! Dennis and I got stuck in to our 'To Do' list with greater conviction over the next few days as we waited for *Caramba* to be fitted out and to receive her Inmarsat communications.

The next day we heard someone calling from the beach. There were a couple of middle-aged women in summer dresses and wide-rimmed fashionable hats waving at us to come to shore. They looked like characters from *Gone with the Wind*. Dennis and I rowed over to see what they wanted.

What interesting people they were. They introduced themselves as members of a group of 50 women who had come to Papeete from New Zealand on a 'Peace Flight' to protest against the tests. The women represented various religious and community organisations as well as Maori and Pacific Island groups. They were a very energetic and enthusiastic pair and vividly described their experiences.

They told us that the group, originally 150 strong, had chartered a Kiwi International plane to take them to Papeete but French officials had revoked the landing rights. The airline was told that if they flew the protest group to Papeete they would face substantial fines from the authorities. The group was also told they would be denied entry. A smaller number, however, still managed to arrive by booking themselves as passengers on the regular commercially scheduled flights to Papeete.

The group had been meeting with various religious, community and political leaders in Papeete and planned other activities to denounce the tests.

We were further inspired by the conviction of this group of New Zealand women. With the arrival of *Sudden Laughter*, *Guinevere*, and *Te Kaitoa* at Papeete, we felt we had enough Moruroa boats to conduct our own protest in the harbour. So on the morning of the 10th of October, four New Zealand flotilla boats donned all banners and flags and began a slow cruise around the perimeter of the harbour. *Joie* led the way, with *Sudden Laughter* next in line followed by *Caramba* and *Te Kaitoa*. John Mate, who was on *Sudden Laughter*, had a megaphone and was shouting "Non a La Bombe, Non a La Bombe", and other French expressions as we went.

One of our key targets was the French frigate *La Nivose*, which was moored at the navy base in the west end of the harbour. She was the same frigate that had seized *Vega* and *Manutea* and harassed the flotilla while at Moruroa. Upon approaching the vessel we were greeted by two inflatables full of French military in uniform and wearing riot gear. We made three passes by the vessel. The French inflatables protected *La Nivose* by moving between her and the protest boats. How ridiculous it seemed! The warship was so large and tall that we could do no harm, let alone board it. Perhaps they thought that we might have a few limpet mines and scuba divers! On the shore riot police took their positions. Tensions rose and our adrenaline levels climbed. Grinning with excitement, Dennis said "Isn't it great to have the Frogs on the defensive for a change?"

The French military obviously took this very seriously and there were no smiling faces. The crew of Zodiacs that flanked us within 3 metres seemed very anxious and would not meet our eyes. At one point, they spoke on a hand-held radio to shore command then donned their bulky belt packs as if they were getting ready to board our boat. The belt packs probably contained teargas, gas masks and other riot control weapons.

I became very nervous and uneasy about what these French madmen might do. We were not in Wellington Harbour; this was a foreign country, one whose government did not like us interfering with their sovereignty. Anything could happen. We were at their mercy. But the four protest boats had strength together and we continued.

An 80-foot harbour patrol boat suddenly appeared and approached *Caramba*. I could see Manuel engaged in a heated conversation with them as they manoeuvred close to the stern. Daniel radioed to us that they had been issued with a citation and that all four boats would get one. As we continued our protest cruise the harbour launch individually approached *Sudden Laughter* and *Te Kaitoa*, issued their citations, then came to us last.

The Polynesian harbour master told us we were 'illegally moving in the harbour without asking permission'. He told us that we must return to our moorage location immediately and that the skippers of the four boats were required to see the Port Captain. The harbour patrol vessel escorted the four boats to the moorage location and did not leave until we were all securely anchored.

I went to the beach to give an interview with the Reuters News Service reporters about the protest. Afterwards, we climbed into a couple of vehicles and drove around to see the Port Captain.

About eleven people went to the office, including the Tahitian activists who had joined us for the protest cruise. When we arrived at the office, the Port Captain said, "Captains only." However, Manuel and Christine (crew of *Sudden Laughter*) insisted on joining us.

The Port Captain was an older Polynesian man with white hair and a pompous attitude and large belly. He was furious with our action and opened the conversation by saying in English, "I am very angry with you all".

Manuel, who spoke a number of different languages fluently and was highly regarded by Greenpeace, stood up to defend the captains. "Why are you angry," he said, "We have done nothing wrong." A long argument then ensued in

French. Manuel would break occasionally to explain to us what the Port Captain was saying.

The Port Captain picked up a thick manual and turned to a clause he had already marked with a highlight pen. The clause said that it was illegal to move in the harbour without port permission, and violators were subject to a $US10,000 fine, and up to 10 days in prison.

We all thought that was ridiculous. Small boats move around in every harbour of the world, including Papeete Harbour, without first asking permission. The rule obviously applied to large cargo vessels and was conveniently being used to keep us under control. The Port Captain informed us that he had been contacted by the French High Commission and told to deal with the situation.

Daniel, who also spoke a little French, asked whether it would have been OK if we had first sought permission to do the protest. Ironically, the Port Captain said no, because they would not have granted us permission! He then said that we would have to return to our yachts and that none of the skippers or yachts were allowed to leave Papeete. We were required to go before a judge next week for sentencing. We and our yachts were under 'boat arrest'.

The tough Port Captain began to soften his stance. He was Polynesian and deep inside we sensed he was sympathetic to our efforts. Most Polynesians were against the nuclear testing. In his role as Port Captain, he was no more than a puppet. He explained to us that he had to follow orders from the French High Commission and he was sorry for that. As we left his office, he gave us each a promotional poster and pamphlet of Papeete Harbour as a gesture of goodwill.

On returning to the Greenpeace office we started to plan ways to address the situation. Dennis and I thought how naive the French authorities were and how they always shot themselves in the foot. If they had done nothing about our little protest, then nothing would have happened. But they are a highly patriotic and emotional bunch and obviously felt that they must respond.

And it was this response that transformed a non-event into international news. Without the inflatables full of commandos, the riot police on the shore, and the subsequent

arrest of our vessels, there would have been nothing
newsworthy to report. Thanks to the French authorities, we
made the front page, second page and third page of their daily
newspaper *Les Nouvelles de Tahiti*. The story also made
international news, especially in New Zealand.

Greenpeace were elated with the positive publicity. Janet
Dalziell told us that it was the best local publicity they had
received since the campaign started. She said that operating in
Papeete was a very hostile environment for Greenpeace and
that the French authorities had managed a propaganda
crusade, blaming them for the riots and social unrest.
Although the press were anti-Greenpeace, they were not anti-
Peace Flotilla. There was no doubt in my mind that this single
harbour protest achieved more result than all our time
protesting at Moruroa. The only people you protested to at
Moruroa were the French military, and they relished the
contention. There were no journalists there to report flotilla
actions.

Concern grew for our safety. The New Zealand Embassy
and Greenpeace lawyers became involved, and there was
international pressure calling for our release. The French High
Commission, already embarrassed by its action, realised that it
would only suffer more damage to its image if it pursued the
prosecutions. Four days later all charges were dropped and we
were free to leave.

We got a lot of publicity from the harbour protest and
subsequent legal affair, but not everyone in Papeete
sympathised with our cause. One evening, shortly after the
event, Dennis was ashore with the dinghy parked on the
beach and I was alone on *Joie*. It was dusk and I saw two men
walking on the beach yelling abusive statements. It appeared
they were yelling to the *Vestorn*, a gallant looking old
Norwegian fishing vessel converted to ocean cruising, which
was anchored next to us. In a North American accent one of
the men was saying, "You bastards. Go home. I will f*ck your
wife."

I did not think much of it and laid down in the aft cabin
for a snooze. I couldn't sleep, however, and got up to rig the
awning when it started to rain. When I looked around, I saw
in the darkness what appeared to be the silhouette of a couple

of coconuts floating together in the water near the bow of
Vestorn. 'This is untypical,' I thought. 'One rarely observes two
coconuts floating together.' I watched the floating objects
closely. They were slowly coming towards me and before long
I could faintly make out that they were human heads; heads
with white faces and short hair, obviously belonging to the
bodies which were underneath the water's surface.

At first I thought it was the crew of *Vestorn* going for a
skinny dip, but it was odd that they were swimming so far out
and in a course towards *Joie*. They were absolutely quiet as
they swam. I suddenly thought these two heads were
swimming towards my boat for sinister reasons. The lights had
been off on *Joie* and the dinghy was ashore. They perhaps
thought the boat was unoccupied and were coming to trash
it.

I slunk below and quietly watched them through the
portlight. When they were within 2 metres of *Joie* I popped up
and said, "Good evening", in a controlled normal voice. There
was no answer. It was very dark, and I could just make out
their expressionless faces. They swam towards the boarding
ladder, which was mounted on the stern of the boat.

With my pulse racing, I reluctantly walked towards the
stern of the boat to challenge them. I had no idea of what was
in store for me. They were only one metre from the boat. I
looked down at them in the dim light and asked, "What are
you guys up to tonight?" There was no answer. At this point I
was sure that these were not your normal casual skinny
dippers. I moved into a position that would allow me to
defend myself by kicking them in the face if they tried to
board *Joie*.

Finally one man began to speak. I recognised his accent
as that belonging to the guy on the beach who was yelling
abuses earlier. "You go near Moruroa again," he said, "and we
will kill the lot of you Kiwi bastards. Do you hear me? We will
put a bomb on your f*cking boat and blow you all up. Do you
hear me?" I nervously replied, "Yes, I hear you."

I could tell by the tone of the man's voice that these guys
were very serious, perhaps out of their trees, and I realised that
in this situation, the best thing I could do was to confuse
them. "But I'm not a Kiwi. I'm American," I said. "You are?"

he asked. "Yes, the boat is from Alaska," I said. This seemed to confuse them and for a moment he hesitated, thinking he might have the wrong boat. However, he continued with his threats and said again that they would kill us all if we went near Moruroa. "You Kiwis and American bastards," he added.

The other guy, who had said nothing at all, did a porpoise dive and swam under the boat, touching the skeg of *Joie*. He then surfaced. I asked him what he put on the boat. They were silent, then began swimming away, repeating their threats, "We will blow you all up." When they were halfway to the shore, the one who did all the talking raised his hand, looked at his watch and said 6.38. I looked at my watch. It was 6 p.m.

This whole event, of course, made me extremely nervous. Were these guys just some drunken legionnaires blowing off steam or did they really put something under *Joie* that would go off at 6.38 p.m.? I watched them as they swam away. When they reached shore, they ran away very quickly. 'Are they running from the imminent explosion?' I thought. I couldn't take any chances so I stripped off my T-shirt and shorts, grabbed my underwater torch and my mask and prepared to go in.

Dennis was just arriving back with the dinghy. He saw me rushing around in the nude and in a panic getting ready to go in. He asked, "What the hell are you doing?" "Going for a swim," I said. "You're crazy! At this time of night?" he asked. I briefly explained what had just happened, and suggested that they may have put a limpet mine under the boat. "I have to check it out right now," I said. I dived in and conducted a thorough inspection of the yacht underwater while Dennis rowed around inspecting the topside.

To my relief, there was nothing. After I explained the story to Dennis in detail, he took the matter quite seriously and rowed over to *Vestorn* to ask if they had been approached. They had not. He then went to the Greenpeace office just across the street and told them of the threats.

Quentin, one of the Greenpeace guys, came out and gave me a cellphone to use. He said he would try to track down Ingrid and John, our prospective crew members to Moruroa, so that they could come aboard and help keep watch during the night.

On Greenpeace's advice, we decided not to report the matter to the police. They believed that the police would use the event to further their propaganda campaign against Greenpeace and the Flotilla. They could blow the whole thing out of proportion. We could imagine the press headlines: 'ANGRY LOCALS THREATEN KIWI PROTESTERS'.

Instead, we posted watches at the Greenpeace headquarters and on *Joie*. John Frost and Ingrid Gordon came out to spend the night on *Joie* and to help keep a night watch. We got to know them while in Papeete and they had signed on as crew for our trip back to Moruroa.

John was a fisherman from Blenheim. He was around 26 years old, tall and fit. He seldom wore a shirt and had long hair always tucked back and held into position under a baseball cap. John was a very quiet person, whose real agenda always seemed vague. He was almost indifferent at times, as if living in another world. His face was stern and tough looking. He did not smile often, and he gave off an atmosphere of having a trigger-happy personality: someone who could easily snap, then instantly remove your head from your body!

Ingrid was John's opposite, and it did not take long to understand that they had a little thing going on together. She loved to talk and socialise. She was a tough woman, somewhat tomboyish, in her early thirties, and a staunch Greenpeace activist. She was very active on the West Coast of America as a front-line activist co-ordinator. She was selected to go to Moruroa on *Manutea* because of her experience and her ability to operate high-powered Zodiacs; and that was how she arrived in French Polynesia.

It was good to have these two valiant people on board now. We speculated as to whether the legionnaires would return and in what form: from the north in a speedboat, underwater with diving apparatus, or in larger numbers from the shore.

They returned at 1 a.m. in the middle of a rainstorm. The same two guys parked their car on the road and the guy with the North American accent repeated his threats, yelling from the shore, "You American and Kiwi bastards, we will blow you up and kill you like we did the *Rainbow Warrior*."

I called the Greenpeace office on the cellphone. Quentin ran outside and was able to get their license plate number. At the same time we noticed a lot of police in the area. They had obviously caught wind that there was something going on, no doubt from the tapped Greenpeace telephones or scanners they used to listen to cellphones.

John Frost became furious as we all listened to the abuse and threats flowing from the shore. He insisted that we inform the police. He said, "There has been a threat on our lives, and no matter whether they are a couple of drunk legionnaires or not, we should inform the police." We debated the matter for some time amongst ourselves and with Greenpeace. Greenpeace maintained the view that it should not be reported to the French Police.

There were no further actions by the men, but they did achieve the effect of keeping us up all night. No one could sleep after the events and we were all bleary eyed in the morning.

Chapter 10

Back to Moruroa! Campaign Close-out

Dennis and I were even more anxious to get out of Papeete as soon as possible. *Caramba* was nearly ready to go and on October 18 we were all set to leave.

David Carline, a representative of the indigenous Koumo people of Southwest Queensland, Australia, and two Tahitians, Guy (Jacqui) Taero and Moorai Ngpao, joined as crew on *Caramba*. Carline initially went to Papeete as a member of an Aboriginal and Torres Strait Islander Peace Delegation. He wanted to travel to Moruroa to bear witness on behalf of the Quaker Friends and to show Aboriginal solidarity with the indigenous people of Polynesia. Taero and Ngpao were veterans of a number of protests at Moruroa.

Also on board *Caramba* were Hans Monker from the Netherlands (radio operator), John Mate from Canada (campaign co-ordinator), and Daniel Mares from New Zealand (skipper). The *Joie* crew consisted of Dennis, John Frost, Ingrid Gordon and me.

That morning Dennis and I walked down town to complete the vessel and crew departure clearance. The customs officer asked us which port we would be clearing for. I said Rarotonga, and Dennis qualified that by saying we would be going back to Moruroa first, then on to Rarotonga.

The officer broke out laughing. He was also a Polynesian and was sympathetic to our cause. He said, "I admire your honesty. Most other yachties would not tell me if they were going to Moruroa. Good luck, and have a good trip," he said. His parting words were, "Watch out for the approaching hurricane season."

We said our goodbyes on the beach to the Greenpeace people and others. The crews rowed out to their respective yachts, pulled anchor, raised sails and we were under way to Moruroa. We were expecting the 660 nautical mile beat directly into the south-easterly trade winds to be a tough sail. However, we would be sailing with *Caramba* and expected some fun and comradeship along the way.

John, our new crew member, had sailed to Moruroa initially as crew on *Sudden Laughter*, but decided to stay in Papeete to further the cause in any way that he could. John initiated the 'Peace Scroll' in his home town of Blenheim. On the scroll were thousands of signatures against French nuclear testing. On his arrival in Papeete, John and the crew of *Sudden Laughter* delivered the scroll to the French High Commission. John told us that the High Commissioner had been 'unavailable' to accept the scroll, so his assistant had accepted it. His assistant told them that he admired their courage of sailing all the way to Moruroa but that it would not make any difference!

Ingrid was an experienced sailor and Greenpeace activist. She was a member of the first action when *Manutea* arrived on scene at Moruroa. She and three other activists went into Moruroa in a Zodiac. When they were captured they claimed they came from *Rainbow Warrior*, which had been confiscated 2 days earlier by the French military. They explained they had been hiding on the island for the last 2 days. The French officers eventually accepted their story, then sent them to Papeete and released them without charges. Ingrid went back to the United States but had returned to French Polynesia for further campaign work.

Daniel had assembled quite an international crew on *Caramba*. He explained how his two Tahitian crew members, Jacqui and Moorai, had spent many years in jail as a consequence of their protests against French sovereignty over their land. A number of people supporting independence from the French had been either put in jail or exiled from Tahiti to France.

The weather was beautiful on our departure from Tahiti. In fact, the winds were so light that we had to motor-sail most the night to our rendezvous point with *New Zealand Maid*.

New Zealand Maid was returning from Moruroa with Jon Tucker, Audrey Cardwell (Greenpeace campaign co-ordinator) and crew on board. They had been at Moruroa for about a week and were the only vessel there.

We were in radio contact with them and planned to meet in the lee of a small island called Mehetia, 90 miles east of Papeete. *New Zealand Maid* would transfer her hand-held Inmarsat telephone to us and her Zodiac to *Caramba*.

It was good to see them all. While the two Greenpeace campaign co-ordinators met on *Caramba* to discuss tactics, Jon rowed over to give us the satellite telephone and portable generator. He was always such a pleasant person, with a large smile. He was happy to see us and instructed us on how to use the hand-held phone.

He told us that the French military were definitely not impressed to see them return. Being the sole protest yacht put them in an extremely vulnerable position, yet they did not feel desperately threatened. They made it clear from the outset via the VHF radio that they intended peaceful protest in international waters. Their strategy was simple: sail a 40-mile south-west/north-east picket line day and night just outside the 12-mile zone.

Although the French blanketed their every move, he said they basically did not hassle them. The most satisfying act of their stay was hoisting a banner on the starboard side of *New Zealand Maid* that read 'HONTE' (French for 'SHAME'). Not a single warship or helicopter would pass them on the offending side. Approaching from astern they would invariably sheer away to port. Jon said that of all the actions, the French military's deliberate avoidance of seeing a single word proved best to them that their protest had an impact.

This illustrates that perhaps the most effective protest flag to wave was their own conscience, from which they judge themselves to be wrong.

We said our goodbyes and hoisted sail for Moruroa. It was another 570 nautical miles to the south-east, a 4-day sail. The wind had freshened a little from the north-east and there was only a small ocean swell, offering ideal sailing conditions. We were slightly faster than *Caramba* and by nightfall they were out of sight. *Caramba* was a longer and bigger yacht, which frustrated Daniel. He tried in vain to catch up with us. So, the race to Moruroa was on!

When we were about 2 days away from Moruroa, we were buzzed regularly by a jet plane. It made two passes each time, at low altitude, just above our masthead. Our protest philosophy was different this time around. Rather than 'brown-eyeing' the French military, we decided to go down below every time they approached, not giving them the opportunity to photograph us and detect who was on board. This keep them guessing and frustrated them immensely. They could not ascertain if we carried more Greenpeace or Tahitian activists ready to breach the Exclusion Zone. "This will keep the power in our court", Dennis said. He suggested this strategy to the *Caramba* crew, who rejected it. None of the their crew had been to Moruroa earlier in the campaign, and thus could not understand the significance of what Dennis proposed. John Mate's and Daniel's point of view was that we were going to Moruroa to bear witness only, and that trying to frustrate the French was not relevant.

The north-easterlies continued and we had 4 days of wonderful sailing. The sun really had a bite to it so for shelter we tied on a large tarpaulin from the back stays to the side stays. Dennis jacked up a pipe affair to feed wind into the boat and we had cushions lying about on deck. The boat looked like a travelling Bedouin camp!

When we arrived at Moruroa, Dennis said, "Well, we made it back home! It actually seems remote when all you can see is sea, sea, sea. Hard to envisage that we are so close to where they let these horrendous f*cking things off! It really is the low point of humanity, these things. And the people who need them do nothing for our progress."

The French warship *La Moqueuse* greeted us by steaming at very close range (15 metres) by both *Caramba* and *Joie*. I called the warship up on VHF channel 16 and warned the skipper that his action was irresponsible and dangerous and to remind him that he was in international waters. I requested that he leave us alone and sail back to Moruroa. No one from the warship responded.

The French forces treated us much more aggressively this time and Daniel and John Mate were beginning to appreciate the significance of the tactical strategies that Dennis had been suggesting earlier. The French were expecting to detonate bomb number three without the annoyance of a Peace Flotilla, and we were back. We could sense their utter frustration with us. They were in pre-test mode and this was definitely 'snap a boat' time.

With the north-easterlies continuing the weather at Moruroa was beautiful. It was hot and sunny, and the seas were calm. It was completely different from the strong south-easterly conditions that had predominated at our first stay. We had more time to relax and go for swims. We hoped that the water was not radioactive.

Interestingly, swimming did not cool us down. The water temperature was actually warmer than the air. I wondered if this was normal, or whether the nearby atoll, which was festering from two recent nuclear explosions, was actually heating up the water! When we got out we were just as hot, if not hotter, than before. But it was good fun swimming in the clear, calm ocean.

We also made a new friend that we named 'Gaffy' – a 6-foot shark. He became our pet shark and had an amazing nose for us, following us around all the time we were there. He swam behind the boat and we would feed him mouldy bread and salami. When we sailed to another location around the atoll, sometimes as much as 20 miles away, Gaffy would show up again several hours later. He really liked the salami and would put his head out of the water to have a better sniff of it.

Gaffy got his name when John Frost put a large piece of salami through the hook on the end of our gaff to feed him. When John reached out with the gaff to present the salami, Gaffy came out of the water and grabbed the salami, gaff hook, and all. He thrashed around so fiercely that John could not hold on. Away he went with the whole lot. Shortly after, he surfaced again without the gaff hook. We hoped he had not swallowed it. Imagine the indigestion!

John, who loved to live on the fringe, got bold one day and decided to go for a swim with Gaffy. There wasn't much else exciting to do out there. You couldn't go out to a party, or to the movies or that sort of thing. Gaffy was not very interested in John, probably because he did not smell like salami! But when Gaffy started swimming straight for him, John had a sudden change of plans. With his adrenaline pumping, he streaked back to the boat as fast as he could and quickly scurried up the boarding ladder, screaming all the way. Just in time! Gaffy was already at his heels. 'What we do for fun and amusement out here,' I thought as we all laughed our guts out.

October 23

It was a new moon and pitch black outside. It was 2 a.m. local time and a French warship was cruising in circles around us, running with all lights off in international waters. We could not see her but could hear the distinctive sound of her massive engines. Maritime law prohibits ships from cruising in international waters at night without lights, especially in times of peace. I gave the vessel six warnings – three first on VHF channel 16, then the rest on SSB radio channel 4417 so that the whole world could hear. "Calling the French warship, the French warship, you are sailing around us in international waters with your lights off. This is in breach of maritime law, and a dangerous act. Please state your intentions, and turn your lights on." They disregarded all attempts to communicate and continued circling us all night at close range like wolves.

At 9 a.m. local time I heard five gun blasts coming from the warship about 3 miles away. The French crew fired two short blasts in succession twice, then a single one. They were trying to intimidate us, and it was working!

We had given a nickname to the French warship *La Moqueuse*. We called her '*La More Cheese*'.

The next evening was very exciting. *Joie* and *Caramba* were floating about 2 miles from the line. We had just finished dinner and it was pitch black outside with no moonlight whatsoever. Ingrid, who went out on deck, heard the faint sound of an outboard engine at idle. She searched the darkness with her small torch, then shouted out in an alarming voice, "Inflatable coming alongside." I popped my head out of the companionway and could dimly see four men in an inflatable wearing black combat gear. They were only 5 metres away from us. 'Something sinister was about to happen,' I thought to myself.

I raced down below to get the search light. I plugged it in and sprang to the deck and turned it on in the direction Ingrid was pointing. The four French soldiers, who had sneaked up in the dark, were blinded by the 1000-candlepower beam and held their arms up to cover their eyes. We saw one hold up what appeared to be a special infrared camera and he took a picture of the front end of *Joie*. We yelled out to them, "What are you doing", and they sped away in the dark. We did not know what they were up to, but all our adrenaline levels were peaking. We lost them temporarily in the dark, but after scanning the horizon with the spot light, we found them again. They were headed full speed for *Caramba* who were a quarter of a mile away.

I gave the search light to John, who was very excited by now, and I told him to hold the light on them. I jumped down and radioed to *Caramba*, "Inflatable approaching your vessel, inflatable approaching your vessel." Dennis yelled, "We need to get over there quick to assist them!" It dawned to us that they may have been trying to sneak up to the Greenpeace boat *Caramba* to seize it, and in the pitch black had mistaken our boat for theirs.

I started the engine expeditiously and we gave pursuit at full throttle, 7.5 knots. John kept the search light on them as they approached *Caramba*. The *Caramba* crew came out on deck with their spot lights, and waited in anticipation for the French Commandos to arrive.

Just before they reached *Caramba* they turned sharply to the left and sped away back to their warship, which was drifting close by with her lights off. It was apparent that they had abandoned their mission, whatever it was. We gave pursuit, but they were much faster. We held the light on them but they quickly pulled away and disappeared into the darkness. That night both vessels maintained a strict 24-hour watch, with buckets of water, oars and lights handy.

The next morning we met on *Caramba* and pondered why the French military tried such an antic. There were a multitude of possible reasons and we narrowed them down.

They may have wanted to seize *Caramba*. This was a Greenpeace vessel with Inmarsat communications on board.

They had already seized three other Greenpeace vessels in international waters. One more would not worry them. If this was their intention, which was foiled, then it was likely that the third nuclear explosion in the test series was imminent.

Another possible reason for the night visit was to take pictures of the crew on deck to see if other people or equipment were on board and/or to determine the best way to board the vessels for a later exercise.

Finally, they may have wanted to slash our Zodiac and communications thus crippling us, or just use scare tactics to harass and exhaust us.

We concluded that something very sinister was going on. Dennis added that the French military were much more aggressive than during our previous stay and that we should prepare for the worst. The French activities included steaming at high speed close by us with their megatonne warships in international waters; circling us at night at close range with all lights off; the shooting of five rounds at sea within earshot of us; and their secret night visit in an inflatable with four commandos.

On many occasions, Daniel and I, as skippers of our respective vessels, called the warships and cited them on their breach of international safety laws. We asked them to turn on their lights or not to pass so close to our vessels as these were negligent, dangerous and unnecessary actions. They did not respond to any of our radio communications and continued with their harassment campaign against us.

A letter was drafted and faxed to the Greenpeace office in Papeete. We asked them to notify the respective consulates of the *Joie* and *Caramba* crew, and to inform them of our imminent danger. This in itself was a bit of a publicity campaign on our part, as the consulates of six different countries would have to be notified. That night 'La More Cheese' had her running lights on!

The next morning both boats sailed to within metres of the line to entice the French warship to our location. We were conscious that the French authorities needed only a small opportunity to snap *Caramba*, so they would come. 'La More Cheese' took the bait. When she steamed close, John Mate and Moorai quickly jumped into the Zodiac and gave pursuit.

What an awesome sight it was to see the two men in a small Zodiac chasing a giant warship through ocean swells! John was at the bow of the Zodiac waving a piece of paper in his right hand and holding on for dear life with his left. He intended to deliver the letter to the warship. It was a letter to Chirac, explaining why we were there. He wanted to give it to the captain for him to read and pass on to Chirac.

John had a hand-held radio and was hailing the warship to halt. Daniel supported him using *Caramba*'s ship radio explaining to the warship what they intended. As the Zodiac approached, the warship flashed her deck lights, tooted her siren, then sped away at top speed. The Zodiac could not match her speed in the ocean swells.

A short time later we were circled by the frigate *Vendemiaire*. John and Moorai used the opportunity to try it again, and received the same response. Daniel again supported the action over the ship's radio and asked permission to deliver the letter.

As the frigate entertained us at close range, we noticed their jet plane making low altitude passes on the line. It flew back and forth over and over again, only metres from the water, as another frigate stood close by. This was something we had not seen them do before, and possibly was an indication that they were about to detonate Number Three.

We had them puzzled as to why we were currently 8 miles off the line. They were probably acting on the suspicion that we had sent a Zodiac in or that one was on the line waiting to go in. We learned from our earlier experiences that the French warships could not easily pick up small craft on their radars, especially if they were made from rubber or plastic.

Another possible explanation was that they were searching for a submarine. Someone leaked a rumour in Papeete (not that it would be the Greenpeace office) that the Peace Flotilla had a small submarine. At least we could rely on the French officials to be very gullible!

The theory that the French Government would soon be detonating Number Three was supported by the fact that Chirac had announced at the 50th anniversary gathering of the United Nations that they would have only three to four more blasts and then stop and sign the 'fully' Comprehensive Test Ban Treaty. Furthermore, France, Britain and the United States agreed they would ratify the South Pacific Nuclear-free Zone Treaty. This was a clever move by Chirac and his allies, as the European Commission was proposing a court order that would have stopped French testing until the environmental effects of their first two tests could be assessed.

Jim Bolger's speech to the UN indicated a softening of his stance against the French tests. He widened the nuclear debate to other concerns such as Chinese testing, the banning of the production of uranium and plutonium, and for further cuts in nuclear arsenals. He also came under pressure from British Prime Minister John Major, who was concerned that the UK would be singled out at the Commonwealth Heads of Government meeting in Auckland in November for not denouncing the French test series.

Apparently Bolger had been sucked into the strategy supported by the big three nuclear powers. He backed down on his opposition to the tests and accepted the French Government's decision to finish the series. This effectively ended New Zealand's protest to the tests. So the light was green again for France to go ahead with four more tests immediately.

How did all this make us feel? We were 12 miles away from an imminent nuclear explosion. We were sacrificing our time, energy and resources in our commitment to stopping the series; playing somewhat pretentious 'cat and mouse' games with an ostentatious French navy. We had been abandoned by the rest of the world. Even our home country Prime Minister had deserted us. He probably did not even know we were still at the line trying to kick some French butt.

The view by the Peace Flotilla was that the pact should be signed now. Why wait for four more tests? John Mate put it this way: "It's like a serial rapist saying he'll only rape four more times, then stop and be a good neighbour." It was absurd, but the world seemed to be falling for it, hook, line and sinker!

Disappointment and frustration had set in amongst the *Caramba* and *Joie* crews. We were down in spirit. Dennis reported that he had called a number of radio stations in New Zealand using *Caramba*'s telephone, but nobody wanted to hear. We had been so isolated that we did not realise the issue was 'old hat' in New Zealand. Dennis said, "good ol' Bolger is saying 'good show chaps, let them have four more!' Why don't the f*cking French just get on and let the bloody thing off so we can go home?" That was the strange sort of dilemma which tore at us all. No one wanted the bomb to go off, but once the sinister act was done, we were free to sail home.

With that, Dennis got motivated to put a large 'HONTE' sign on our sail. He had talked about doing it since we arrived at Moruroa, but kept putting the job off. Some instinct made him decide it must be done now or never. I gave him a hand. We pulled the sail down, laid it out on the deck and with a pencil and a roll of duct tape inscribed the word. When we raised the sail again, the bold 10-foot 'HONTE' was there to shame the French military. It was a little act, but it made Dennis and I feel as if we had done something special to protest against the imminent test.

BOOM! – French Explosion Number Three
October 27, 1995: they did it! A 60-kilotonne nuclear explosion (four times the size of the bomb dropped over Hiroshima) was detonated only 12 miles from us. We could feel a shuddering through the hull as the shock wave hit us, then there was a prolonged vibration and a rushing, roaring noise.

It was quite an emotive time for everybody. None of us had ever been next door to a nuclear explosion. We all sat around sort of stunned, looking at each other, saying obvious things, not sure what to say or how to feel. Our anger turned to remorse. Our eyes moistened with tears. It was a strange feeling, one that I had never experienced. We were consumed by the realisation that there was nothing we could do about it, and so it would happen regardless. I would imagine it to be like the feeling one has when a beloved one has been sentenced by a court of law to death; a feeling of hopelessness and anger with the system. And then the day comes. Your loved one is executed. You loose someone very special. You are very empty and sad. What a waste. What was the point of it all anyway?

The crew of *Caramba* and *Joie* agreed earlier that we

would leave soon after the French conducted the third test. We would bear witness, then have a campaign closing ceremony. The hurricane season was already upon us.

As part of the ceremony, I pulled out our French courtesy flag, dowsed it with kerosene and burnt it in front of a passing French frigate. The captain tooted his horn in anger. I announced the action over the radio and said that I burnt the flag not in protest against the French people, but rather their government who had continued with the nuclear bomb madness. They had pressed on with complete arrogance and total disregard for the rest of the world, as well as their own people who had asked them to stop the tests.

The crew of *Caramba* then gave their closing campaign speeches over the VHF radio. John Mate, the Greenpeace campaign co-ordinator, said many of the things he had said in the past; "Shame on Chirac, Shame on France. This is an atrocity to mankind which the whole world is against." Daniel, the skipper, came on next and said what a sad moment it was for him. The two Tahitians on board, Jacqui and Moorai, gave a quick word and said goodbye. Then Dave, the Aborigine from Australia, spoke. He choked in sadness and could not finish his sentence. He was crying. What a sensitive man he was. He expressed sadness for the Polynesian people who had been struggling for their lands for many years and said he was also sad to be saying goodbye to the *Joie* crew. Hans, the radio operator, finished off with a similar short speech and said goodbye to all of us.

It was our turn. Dennis started off by expressing his deep sorrow, then in his philosophical manner explained why we came and what we had accomplished. He said that he was afraid that anger, bitterness and hate would be his strongest feelings, but they weren't. He said he did not hate the French Government and wished he could speak with the French sailors and air crew who were on the vessels which patrolled us. "I would like to ask them what their view and feeling was. Perhaps they didn't believe in the bomb either and were just following orders. Perhaps there is still some hope."

John Frost took his turn next, and started by playing a solo on his pan pipes. He played it with conviction and sadness. He closed with a few sentimental words. Ingrid, our last crew member, was next and then I finished off.

It was not usually easy for me to speak on an emotional level, but words seemed to flow on this occasion. I started by saying thanks to *Caramba* and crew for their support throughout the campaign. "I don't know exactly how I feel at the moment, but I am very empty. There is a feeling of sadness in me, torn by anger. We may have lost the battle here at Moruroa, but there is a small glowing feeling deep inside of me that is growing and saying we will win the war. I feel the greatest sadness for the Polynesian people, who have been treated with little respect throughout the French occupation of these beautiful islands. If the French Government is true to their word and sign the Treaty of Rarotonga for a Nuclear-free Pacific, then perhaps there is a chance for these people to gain their independence and lead their own lives proudly and with glory. I feel for them. Goodbye to *Caramba* and crew. This is *Joie* out."

The last remaining Peace Flotilla vessels, the *Joie* and the *Caramba*, left Moruroa. *Caramba* set sail on a north-west course back to Papeete, and *Joie* went due west to Rarotonga. In 2 hours we lost sight of each other.

We said goodbye to Gaffy, and goodbye to Moruroa. Even though Moruroa was a desolate place, abused many times over by the French Government and festering with three more nuclear explosions, it was a place which we had learnt to accept as our temporary home. It was a strange feeling to finally be leaving after all this time.

A French frigate followed us for 3 hours then finally turned back, accepting that we had actually left. They were probably disappointed to see us go. There would be little for them to do without flotilla boats to keep track of, to harass and wave their big stick at.

Our sadness and remorse slowly dissipated. It was replaced by a feeling of relief that it was all over. We had a new challenge: sailing 3000 nautical miles back to New Zealand.

Campaign closed. We were on our way home!

EPILOGUE

Joie and crew made an 11-day passage to Rarotonga in the Cook Islands. The weather was most odd for the first 3 days after leaving Moruroa. It was very balmy with intense and peculiar electrical storms. We suspected that the nuclear explosion had affected the local weather patterns. We spent 5 days reprovisioning and doing odd repairs in Rarotonga before making the next long passage to New Zealand, arriving in Auckland on the 24th of November. As expected, getting back into New Zealand was bouncy; we arrived in the company of a 45-knot gale, and a number of new sailing yarns. All in all, we were gone from New Zealand for 3 months, spending all but 15 days at sea, and over 30 days on site at Moruroa and nearby Tureia. *Joie* was the longest-staying New Zealand Peace Flotilla boat at Moruroa.

We arrived unannounced in Auckland at midnight. The only people there to greet us were Customs and Immigration officials. They were not in a particularly good mood after being called out into the gale force conditions so late at night. It was an odd arrival. We were the last boat returning, and we sensed the mood of the media and public had changed. The tests were no longer an important public issue, we were the last returning flotilla vessel and, after being away for three months, had been largely forgotten.

After our clearance, Dennis and I decided to go out on the town and celebrate our return to New Zealand before the pubs closed. Our spirits were dampened after we were turned away from pub after pub due to our scruffy appearance. Even when we announced that we had just arrived from Moruroa, it made no difference; we were sent on our way. We returned to the *Joie* and looked forward to our sail back to Wellington harbour, 800 nautical miles down the coast, where our dedicated supporters were anxiously awaiting our return in early December.

The reality of being back in the 'real world' had begun to sink in. The following day I checked my bank account to find unsurprisingly that there was no money in it. The donations made by the New Zealand public helped immensely, but still they covered only about half of the direct expense of the trip. I met with the other shareholders of my New Zealand business while in Auckland. They were very disappointed and unsympathetic that I had left the business for such a long time. They took legal action, which resulted in the loss of my business. With no income, or other immediate prospects for a job, I joined the dole queue. I had thought that my situation was atypical but, after speaking with other returning skippers, I discovered that most also suffered financial hardship.

Although I had lost much in doing the trip, I had gained a worthy and memorable experience and, most importantly, a good friend. Dennis learned to be an excellent sailor and we bonded through the experiences and time we shared together. We have been best friends ever since.

More than 30 different vessels from twelve different countries visited Moruroa to protest. Some spent only hours at the location, and some tried but never made it there. Despite earlier reports of some 40 boats coming from Australia, not one made it. Of the 14 New Zealand Peace Flotilla yachts, all made the 6000 nautical mile ocean passage to Moruroa and back without major incident.

Yachts that protested at Moruroa★

Anna	New Zealand Peace Flotilla
Aquila d'Oro	New Zealand Peace Flotilla
Chimera	New Zealand Peace Flotilla
Guinevere	New Zealand Peace Flotilla
Gemini Galaxsea	New Zealand Peace Flotilla
Joie	New Zealand Peace Flotilla
Kela	New Zealand Peace Flotilla
New Zealand Maid	New Zealand Peace Flotilla
Photina	New Zealand Peace Flotilla
Pickety Witch	New Zealand Peace Flotilla
R Tucker Thompson	New Zealand Peace Flotilla
Sudden Laughter	New Zealand Peace Flotilla

Triptych	New Zealand Peace Flotilla
Te Kaitoa	New Zealand Peace Flotilla
Tui	New Zealand Government Research Ship
Suilven	Ocean Ferry en route from Scotland to New Zealand
Bebinka	Chile
Te-Au-O-Tonga	Cook Islands
Matagi Princess	Cook Islands
Bifrost	Denmark
Tau	Fiji
Kidu	France
Tara	Germany
Pozzuolana	Germany
Lady Sephora	Germany
Aveia	US
Machias	US
Regulus Star	Tahiti
Moira	Tahiti
Lelitka	Ukraine
Caramba	Greenpeace Vessel
MV Greenpeace	Greenpeace Vessel
La Ribaude	Greenpeace Vessel
Manutea	Greenpeace Vessel
Rainbow Warrior	Greenpeace Vessel
Vega	Greenpeace Vessel

★List derived from Auckland Peace Flotilla Office media reports. One or two boats listed may not have actually reached Moruroa.

APPENDIX

After the Peace Flotilla

France finished the test series at Moruroa, in the face of world-wide condemnation, because the tests were 'irrevocable'. President Chirac did, however, cut the number of tests from eight to six, finishing 4 months ahead of schedule.

The fourth test, a 40-kilotonne explosion, was conducted only 5 days after the UN General Assembly called for an 'immediate cessation of all nuclear testing' and just a week after the Commonwealth Heads of Government Meeting, held in Auckland, debated the issue. The sixth and largest test, 120 kilotonnes, was detonated on 27 January 1996, coincidentally during the reunion of the Moruroa Peace Flotilla at Kawau Island, north of Auckland. The French authorities subsequently admitted radioactive iodine-131 had been released.

In February 1996, Jacques Chirac reasserted that nuclear deterrence remained the fundamental principle behind France's defence strategy and the test series was required to modernise France's nuclear arsenal and to allow them to conduct nuclear computer simulation.

In March, the French released all five captured Greenpeace vessels and helicopter, after holding them for up to 5 months.

A month before the end of the French test series, the leaders of Brunei, Indonesia, Malaysia, the Philippines, Singapore, Thailand and Vietnam declared South-East Asia a nuclear weapons-free zone. The treaty outlawed possession, manufacture and acquisition of nuclear weapons in the zone.

On the 26th of March, 1996, the South Pacific officially became a nuclear-test-free zone with the signing in Suva of the protocols to the South Pacific Nuclear-free Zone Treaty by France, Britain and the United States. The three nuclear powers' endorsement of the treaty came 11 years after it was first signed by several South Pacific Forum countries, and only months after the last French test at Moruroa. The protocols pledge the countries not to manufacture or station nuclear weapons within territories they were responsible for and not to test nuclear devices in the zone. They also pledged not to use or threaten to use nuclear weapons within the zone.

In July, the 15 UN judges of the World Court issued a decision that made the use or threat of nuclear weapons illegal in warfare, except perhaps in self defence.

Finally, the Comprehensive Test Ban Treaty was signed after five decades of nuclear testing. The 50th UN General Assembly overwhelmingly approved the CTBT on 10 September 1996 and it was signed 16 days later. The UN countries agreed on a 'zero yield' comprehensive test ban, meaning that all nuclear tests of any size were banned. This was a significant achievement.

From the first nuclear test in 1945 (an 18.5-kilotonne atmospheric test at Alamogordo, New Mexico) to the date of signing of the CTBT, there had been 2046 nuclear tests at more than 20 locations around the world by six different nations. This averages out at nearly one test every 9 days.

When I returned to New Zealand after the campaign, a few people suggested that I had wasted my time, money and energy, and that the Peace Flotilla had accomplished nothing; the French had still gone on with their tests. Although we were not able to stop the tests, we succeeded in disrupting, delaying and forcing changes to the French Government's plans. Clearly, the importance of the Peace Flotilla had been as the focal point of the international campaign against the nuclear testing. Because we were out there, we became a motivational force for the rest of the world to join in in any way that it could, and people did so by the millions, in the most creative ways possible.

There is no question in my mind that the Flotilla, which consisted of ordinary men, women and children, made a direct contribution to worldwide political thinking and against nuclear proliferation. This assisted in the overwhelming political support and speed of adoption of the ASEAN Nuclear-free Zone, the South Pacific Nuclear-free Zone, the Comprehensive Test Ban Treaty, and to some degree the World Court judgement that nuclear weapons were basically illegal, all of which transpired within months of the Peace Flotilla campaign close-off. Our protest also attracted worldwide attention to the Chinese, who were also testing during that same period.

The challenge, however, is still not over and the threat of nuclear weaponry advancement is still rife. France has demonstrated this by its ambitious nuclear development programme. Despite ratifying the Comprehensive Test Ban Treaty, it plans to build a number of new facilities (including a megajoule laser for weapons research in the thermonuclear field) and aims to develop and deploy at least two further nuclear warheads over the next decade.

Nuclear testing will not stop. Non-nuclear weapons states will push for nuclear weapons status and power (witness Pakistan and India). Furthermore, testing will change form, from physical testing to laboratory computer simulation, out of the public eye and most difficult to monitor or contest.

New nuclear weapons are under development as I write. Furthermore, there are major concerns about the safety, ownership and control of the huge stockpiles of ageing nuclear bombs. These have sufficient combined force to destroy our civilisation many times over.

Then there is the issue of the Moruroa and Fangataufa atolls. They were once small tropical paradises but are now diseased, festering with the contamination of some 193 nuclear explosions. The degree of abuse of these atolls is so great that their very nature has been destroyed. It will be many thousands of years before the effects can subside. What responsibility will the French Government take in restoring these testing grounds?

The French Government initiated an International Atomic Energy Agency study after the series was completed. An international team of scientists spent 2 years investigating the current and future radiological impact of the 193 atmospheric and underground nuclear tests at Moruroa and Fangataufa atolls. The findings seem to contradict the conclusions: the study reported that 5 kilograms of plutonium remained in the sediment of Moruroa's lagoon and a further 3 kilos remained in Fangataufa's lagoon, that there were signs of leakage from cavities created by the underground tests, and there were an estimated 500 kilograms of plutonium in cavities under the atolls. No detailed geological study of the atolls' basalt base was conducted.

Nevertheless the report concluded that there will be 'no radiological health effects' to people, and 'no effects on marine ecosystems' in the lagoons. Therefore 'neither remedial actions nor continuing environmental monitoring at Mururoa and Fangataufa are needed on radiological protection grounds'. This gave France the green light to simply walk away from the contaminated site if it wished.

The study has already been contested by the Independent Research and Information Commission on Radioactivity (CRII-RAD). Their study found that radioactivity was 94 to 371 times above the level required for the sites to be maintained under surveillance and reported that radioactivity was leaking into the water table, lagoons and ocean. In May 1999 the new director of France's Atomic Energy Commission, René Pellet, admitted that there were fractures in the coral at Moruroa and Fangataufa Atolls. Pellet made the admission in Tahiti after carrying out an inspection of the two sites.

In March 2001, a senior scientist in France's nuclear monitoring agency admitted that the rock of Moruroa Atoll was deteriorating because of sustained nuclear testing, and it was reported that entire sections of rock in the atoll's north-east were threatened with collapse. Measurements show they are bulging seawards while the surface of the atoll is compacting. This adds to The International Geomechanical Commission's assessment in mid-1999, when it reported on plutonium 'hotspots' and the risk of part of the atoll collapsing, possibly causing tidal waves.

Finally, there is the question of the Polynesian peoples. There is no denying that the French Government maintained interest in these islands for the benefit of nuclear testing. This has had an overwhelming impact on the socio-economic structures in French Polynesia. Although France has pledged to maintain a certain level of financial support for a 10-year period following the test series, will this be adequate to take French Polynesia through a period of major readjustment? Will France now support a policy of an independent Polynesia, which is no longer subject to the whims of French politicians?

Yes, the worldwide campaign against the French tests was extremely worthwhile and all those who participated should be mighty content with themselves and their contribution. For the safety of our children and generations to follow, I hope that ordinary citizens around the world will continue to take up the many new challenges towards a nuclear weapons-free planet.

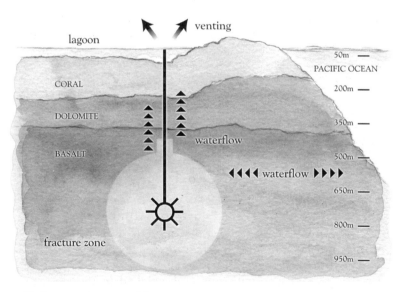

Underground tests at Moruroa are conducted at the bottom of shafts drilled through both the outer rim of the atoll, and the lagoon, down to the basalt core of the atoll to a depth of 500-1200 metres, depending upon the yeild of the device. The French claim that the explosions create cavities similar to glass balls, which prevents leakage of radioactive material. Diagram courtesy of: Greenpeace

Glossary

abeam: at right angles to, or beside, the boat

aft: back part, usually referring to position on the boat

aloft: above the deck, usually up the mast

anti-foul: protective paint put on the bottom of the hull to prevent marine growth

astern: behind the boat

backing (wind): changing of the wind direction, opposite of **veering**: clockwise in southern hemisphere, counter clockwise in northern

backstay: stay (line or cable) used to support the mast; the backstay runs from the masthead to the stern and helps keep the mast from falling forward

beam: boat's widest point, usually near the middle

bearing: direction of an object expressed either as a true bearing as shown on the chart, or as a bearing relative to the heading of the boat

beat: sail to windward

below: under the deck

berth: (1) place for a person to sleep; (2) place where the ship can be secured; (3) safe and cautious distance, e.g. 'We gave the shark a wide berth'

bilge: space between the floor boards and the bottom of the boat, where water and other items accumulate

boom vang: line that adjusts downward tension on the boom

boom tang: metal piece attached to the end of the boom, to which the main sheet line is attached

boom: pivoted spar, with one end attached to the mast, to which the foot of a sail is attached

bow: fore-end of a boat or ship

buoy: anchored float serving as a navigation mark or to show reefs etc.

catamaran: twin-hulled boat; catamaran sailboats can plane and are faster than single-hulled boats (monohulls) in some conditions

chart: map of part of the sea, showing currents, depths, islands, coasts etc.

clew: part of the sail to which the sheets attach

cockpit: sunken well in the middle or back of the boat where the steering wheel and compass are located and where the helmsman and crew usually sit

companionway: opening from which the main cabin is accessed, typically from the cockpit

course: direction taken by a ship; typically magnetic course, or true course.

courtesy flag: small version of the flag of the country being visited; flown from the starboard spreader

cradle: frame to support a vessel when out of water

crest: top of a wave

drogue: any object used to increase the drag of a boat through the water; typically shaped like a parachute or cone opened underwater, drogues slow a boat's motion in heavy weather

east wind, easterly: wind coming from the east

easting: distance travelled or the angle of longitude measured eastward from either a defined north-south grid line or a meridian

EPIRB: Emergency Position Indicating Radio Beacon; an emergency device that uses a radio signal to alert satellites or passing aircraft to its position.

fin keel: keel that is narrow and deeper than a full keel; a full keel runs the length of the boat

fissile matter: material capable of undergoing nuclear fission

flange: metal fitting which attaches the propeller shaft to the engine transmission

forestay: wire support which runs from the top of the mast to the bow; the foresails are attached to the forestay

forward: toward the bow

fouled: entangled or clogged

gaff-rigged: type of traditional working boat using four-sided gaff sails hoisted on gaffs

gaff: (1) spar that holds the top of a four-sided gaff sail; (2) pole with a hook used to land fish

gale: storm with a wind speed between 34 and 40 knots

galley: boat's kitchen area

genoa: large foresail

gooseneck: device connecting the boom to the mast

GPS: Geographical Positioning System; an electronic navigational device which uses satellites to determine its position on Earth

goosewinged: method of running before the wind with two sails set; usually the mainsail on one side and a headsail on the other, or one headsail on each side

halyard: rope or wire which attaches to the top of the sail for hoisting it up the mast

hatch: opening in a boat's deck fitted with a cover

hank: (1) clips used to fasten a sail to a stay; (2) using such clips to attach a sail to a stay

head: (1) top of the sail (2) toilet in a boat

headsail: another term for the front sail

heave-to: to stop a boat and maintain position (with some leeway) by balancing rudder and sail to prevent forward movement; a boat stopped this way is 'hove to'

helm: tiller or wheel that controls the rudder and steers the boat

hoist: raise aloft

hull: body of a boat

inflatable: dinghy or raft that can be inflated for use or deflated for easy stowage

jack stay: strong line, usually of flat webbing, or a wire stay running fore and aft along the sides of a boat to which a safety harness can be attached

jib: small foresail

jibe (accidental): when sailing before the wind, if the helmsman is not careful with the boat's course, or there is a sudden wind change, the mainsail and boom may be blown to the opposite side with such violence that damage may result

jibe (controlled): a controlled jibe is managed by the crew to change course, so that the manoeuvre does not cause any damage

ketch: two-masted ship with a small mast mounted forward of the rudder post

knocked down: when a boat has rolled so that she is lying on her side or even rolled completely over; a boat with appropriate ballast should right herself after being knocked down.

knot: speed through water; the velocity in nautical miles (6080 feet) per hour

latitude: distance north or south of the equator; measured in degrees

lee–cloth: piece of canvas or other material which can be secured down the edge of a bunk to prevent the occupant falling out

leeward: direction away from the wind; in the rules of the road, the leeward boat is the one farthest from where the wind is coming from; also, the leeward side is the downwind side

lifeline: cable fence surrounding the deck; helps prevent crew falling overboard

longitude: distance in degrees east or west of the meridian at Greenwich, England

LPG: liquid petroleum gas; commonly used for cooking and heating on boats

luffing: a flapping motion along the luff (leading edge) of a sail; a sail begins to luff when the air flow stalls when travelling across the sail; luffing is a sign that the sail is not properly trimmed or that the boat is trying to sail too close to the eye of the wind (pinching)

mainsail: the main sail that is suspended from the main mast

mainsheet: line that controls the boom

mast: any vertical pole on the boat that sails are attached to; if a boat has more than one mast, they can be identified by name

motor–sail: use of the motor when sailing to increase the sailboat's performance

nautical mile: measurement used by sailors: 6080 feet (a land mile is 5280 feet)

north wind, **northerly**: wind coming from the north

outrigger: float attached to one or both sides of the hull to help prevent a capsize

painter: short line, typically attached to a dinghy

port: left side of vessel when facing forward

porthole: a port, portlight: window in the side of a boat, usually round or with rounded corners; sometimes portholes can be opened, sometimes they are fixed shut

pounding: impact of the underside of the boat striking a wave; uncomfortable and can cause damage

propeller shaft: spinning shaft from the engine to which the propeller is attached

reaching: sailing with the wind coming from the side

reef: (1) partially lower a sail so that it is not as large; this helps prevent too much sail from being in use when the wind gets stronger; (2) line of rock and coral near the surface of the water

rigging: standing rigging is the mast and support lines, running rigging is the lines with which sails are adjusted

rudder: fin under the stern of the boat used in steering

running lights: lights required to be shown on boats underway between sundown and sunup

running: sailing with the wind directly astern

safety harness: device worn around a person's body that can be attached to jack lines to help prevent a person from becoming separated from the boat

sail track: slot on the mast into which the lugs or sail slides in the luff of the sail are inserted to attach the sail; most masts and roller reefing jibs use sail tracks; systems with two tracks can allow for rapid sail changes

schooner: sailboat with two or more masts; the aft mast is the same size or larger than the forward one(s)

sea cock: through-hull valve, a shut-off on a plumbing or drain pipe between the vessel's interior and the sea

sea room: safe distance from the shore or other hazards

seaworthy: boat or boat's gear able to meet the usual sea conditions

shackle: u-shaped piece of steel with a screw pin which connects across the top to make an enclosed fitting; used for joining many items such as the headsail to the halyard, anchor rode to the anchor line, etc.

sheet: rope attached to the sail for adjusting its angle to the wind; the foresail is controlled by jib sheets, the mainsail by the mainsheet, etc.

shroud and stays: wire or rope lines which support the mast

skeg: any flat protrusion on the outside of the hull that is used to support another object such as the propeller shaft or rudder

skipper: captain of a ship

sloop: style of sailboat with a single mast with one mainsail and one foresail

south wind, **southerly**: wind coming from the south

spreaders: struts used to hold the side stays away from the mast

squall: sudden intense wind storm of short duration, often accompanied by rain; squalls often accompany an advancing cold front

square rigged: sailboat having square sails hung across the mast

SSB Radio: Single Side Band radio; SSB is used for long-distance radio communications, typically 1000 to 5000 miles, sometimes more

stanchion: post near the edge of the deck used to support life lines

starboard: right side of the vessel when facing forward

stern: rear section of the boat

storm jib: small sail which is used in the front of the boat in a strong gale or storm

storm trivial: very strong sail used in stormy weather; it is loose footed, being attached to the mast but not the boom; this helps prevent boarding waves from damaging the sail or the rigging

storm: bad sailing conditions, including rough, high seas and strong winds; probably uncomfortable or dangerous, winds typically above 50 knots

swell: large smooth waves that do not crest; formed by wind action over a long distance

tack: turn the boat's head through the wind so that you sail on the opposite side

tender: small boat used to ferry people and supplies between a larger boat and the shore

tight reaching: sailing into the wind as close as possible

topping lift: line running from the end of the boom to the top of the mast; used to keep the boom from falling when the sail is not set

topsail: triangular sail set above the gaff on a gaff-rigged boat

trimaran: boat with a centre hull and two smaller outer hulls called amas

trough: bottom of a wave, the valley between the crests

true course: direction the boat is travelling expressed in degrees, e.g. 90° true; magnetic course is the course shown on the compass, which is often different due to local compass deviation

vaka: Polynesian canoe with outrigger

vane: flat device that is affected by the wind; used in wind direction indicators and self steering gear systems

VHF radio: radio transmitter and receiver which uses Very High Frequency; VHF only works for short distances, 'line of sight', or up to ~20 miles

wake: waves or turbulence caused by a boat passing through water

watch: (1) division of crew into shifts; (2) the time each watch has on duty

west wind, **westerly**: wind coming from the west

winch: metal drum-shaped device used to wind in the lines that trim the sails.

windward: direction toward the wind; the windward boat is the one closest to where the wind is coming from

whisker-pole: pole with one end attached to the mast while the other end holds the clew of the front sail out so it can catch the wind; used when running down-wind

ALSO AVAILABLE IN THE REED'S MARITIME LIBRARY

ALL FOR A BOTTLE OF WHISKY
Lying buried on Isle of Arran is a bottle of whisky. On the far side of the world a highly pressurized sales manager decides that the time has come for a change of gear. He wants to return to Europe, and instead of taking the plane he finds himself *Ryusei*, a beautiful 44-ft wooden sloop. Together with friends who form a happy gang of 'Three Men in a Boat,' he sets sails. Taking a long route from Asia via Africa and the Americas they head to Scotland — to dig up the whisky.

Ralph von Arnim, born in 1956 of a German father and French mother, is a metallurgist by training. He was working in Asia's steel industry when he opted to interrupt his career to sail home. His ports of call included many a beautiful island and exquisite cove, but also a handful of industrial sites on which he had worked. He, his wife and son are currently at anchor.

SAILING IN GRANDFATHER'S WAKE
Here is a seafaring adventure spanning three generations. In 1938, *Caplin*, skippered by Commander R. D. Graham with his daughter Marguerite as mate, set out from England to sail around the world. Sixty years later, Commander Graham's grandson, Captain Ian Tew, bought *Independent Freedom* in New York and, with his aunt's account of the voyage as a guide, sailed in *Caplin*'s wake. The side-by-side accounts of their navigation to remote shores provide a fascinating historical perspective against which the calms and storms of sailing are ageless.

Born into a seafaring family reaching back to a notoriously successful 17th century privateer, Ian Tew was learning to sail at the age of seven. He made his career in the British Merchant Navy and then as a salvor in the Middle and Far East but, after returning to the UK in 1991 to run a small business, has put to sea again.

SHIPWRECK OR SHANGRI-LA?
Peter Lickfold and his wife Tina decided to follow their dream of buying a boat and sailing from their home in South Africa to Salomon island in the Indian Ocean. *Shipwreck or Shangri-la?* tells the story of their adventures. Shipwrecked on the reef at Boddam, a remote atoll, they were helped by visiting yachtsmen and over a one-year period, they were able to recover their yacht, *Vespera*, and do emergency repairs. They adapted to life in primitive conditions and made the best of it. Sleeping on hammocks, fishing, taking care of their pets, Jess, the cat and Hermie, a hermit crab, was idyllic, but they also had to fight rats, spiders and scorpions. The help they received from the many visiting yachtsmen led to diverging opinions and conflicts. Finally *Vespera* was ready to take them back on a 3000-mile voyage home.

Peter Lickfold was born in 1944 in Franham, England. After starting a career in engineering design, at the age of 28 he emigrated with his wife and three young children to South Africa. In 1989 he abandoned a regular lifestyle and took up sailing. He is now back in South Africa, working as a draftsman in Richards Bay.

SHERIDAN HOUSE
America's Favorite Sailing Books
www.sheridanhouse.com